D1431269

How To Know

THE
FALL FLOWERS

Pictured-Keys for determining the more common fall-flowering herbaceous plants with suggestions and aids for their study.

MABEL JAQUES CUTHBERT

Camp Staff—Audubon Camp of Wisconsin
Visiting Instructor—Central Michigan University

WM. C. BROWN COMPANY PUBLISHERS
Dubuque, Iowa

Library of Congress Catalog Card Number: 49-959

ISBN 0−697−04811−X (Cloth)
ISBN 0−697−04810−1 (Paper)

Eleventh Printing, 1971

THE PICTURED-KEY NATURE SERIES

How To Know The—

Printed in United States of America

INTRODUCTION

n absorbing hobby contributes much toward a person's happiness. Interest in some form of biology is heartily recommended as a restful leisure-time pursuit. It is inexpensive and almost always available; it holds your interest and contributes to healthy outdoor living. To be on familiar terms with each of the world's more than a million species of plants and animals is impossible. However, we can get acquainted with some of them. Learning to recognize many of our more-common fall flowers will prove relatively easy and quite satisfying.

It has been our aim to gather together in this book many of the well known herbaceous fall-flowering plants of southern Canada and the United States east of the Rocky Mountains. Plants cannot always be designated as blooming only in the spring, summer, or fall. Most of the asters, goldenrods, and gentians restrict their blooming to autumn whereas some plants start to flower in the spring or summer months and continue until frost. Representative species from both of these groups are included as well as a few plants which are conspicuous in the fall because of their fruit. Grasses, rushes, sedges, and plants of tropical United States have not been considered.

Over 350 species of fall-flowering plants are keyed and illustrated. Mention is made of others. The range of each species is shown by means of individual distribution maps. Measurements apply to a typical plant of the species.

We have constantly endeavored to choose simple and understandable words often supplementing them with illustrations to further clarify doubtful points. Thus it is hoped that beginners will be encouraged to find lasting pleasure in their study of fall flowers. The more experienced probably will not object seriously to this feature. At no point has scientific reliability or accuracy been knowingly sacrificed for the sake of simplicity.

This book could not have been written without the generous and understanding assistance of Professor H. E. Jaques. Appreciation for helpful advice goes to Dr. Edgar T. Wherry. Others have assisted in various ways. We are grateful to them all.

Mt. Pleasant, Michigan
September, 1948

Mabel Jaques Cuthbert

CONTENTS

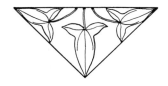

SOMETHING ABOUT PLANTS

Fall is here. It's a time for happy hours outdoors gathering nuts and mushrooms and enjoying the brilliant autumn colors. As we rustle the crisp dry leaves underfoot and breathe the cool tangy air we are conscious of the brightly-hued flowers to be seen in generous profusion. Last spring the pale delicate flowers unfolded into a dull-appearing, often cold world followed by the hardier and more colorful blossoms of summer; but now the woods, roadsides, and streams are dazzlingly bright with vigorous golden-yellow sunflowers, rosinweeds, goldenrods and showy lobelias, gentians, asters. It is nature's final and most prolific flower show before snow flies. Can we afford to miss it?

As a rule most people are better acquainted with spring flowers than with the plants that bloom in the summer and fall. This is quite natural. During the long winter months we have wearied of cold, ice, and snow and are anxious to see green plants again and to get out-of-doors. We remark often about the grass getting greener; about northward-bound birds we have seen; and we eagerly watch for the first blossoms of Spring. Very few of us survive this season without at least a mild enthusiasm for spring flowers.

By the time Fall rolls around we have been out-of-doors on many occasions — swimming, picnicking, boating, hiking, and what not. In the meantime we have unconsciously let plants become part of the background instead of heralding each new blossom as an important event. The fall flowers are just as varied, just as interesting, and just as much fun to know and enjoy as are the better known flowers of Spring.

There are several striking differences between spring flowers as a group and the fall flowers. A large majority of the spring flowers are delicately colored, many of them being pinkish, lavender, pale blue, light yellow, and often white. Intense hues of red, blue, violet, yellow, and orange seem to be dominant among the fall flowers.

1

In the spring we find most of the flowers in wooded areas where they hasten to put forth leaves and blossoms before the overtowering trees and shrubs cut off the sunlight with their later-appearing foliage. Look to the open places for most of the fall flowers — roadsides, fields, prairies, stream banks, and open woods.

Often most of the plants of a family or of some other group confine their blooming period almost entirely to one particular season. A good many plants of the big group Monocotyledonae (which includes the Lily family, the Iris family, the Amaryllis family, the Arum family, and

others) bloom only in the spring. Most of the violets, the phlox, the buttercups and many other members of the family Ranunculaceae are largely spring flowers also. In the fall, the great family Compositae presents in abundance its asters, sunflowers, goldenrods, thistles, burmarigolds, cone flowers, and many others. The gentians and the lobelias are largely fall-blooming as are also many members of the Figwort family.

Maybe you will be able to discover other differences.

We will find it easier and get more satisfactory results in our study of fall flowers if first of all we learn some of the basic facts about plants. For best results in perfecting any new skill — driving a car, baking a cake, building a boat — we prepare for it as adequately as we are able. Thus with this new endeavor, things will go more smoothly if we have the following points in mind.

PLANT GROUPS

All of the world's plants, depending upon their structure, are placed in one of four main divisions. The first three divisions of the plant kingdom include seaweeds, algae, mushrooms, molds, rusts, mildew, bacteria, mosses, liverworts, ferns and their allies. Many of these plants are quite small and none of them produce flowers or seeds.

The members of the fourth division are called Spermatophytes (seed-bearing plants) and are the most highly developed of all; they do produce flowers and seeds. Practically all of our familiar and conspicuous plants are in this seed-bearing group and include trees, shrubs, vines, vegetables, weeds, grasses, sedges, rushes, and flowers of garden, field, and woods.

Plants are *woody* (trees, shrubs, and many vines) or *herbaceous* (soft-stemmed). The cells of woody plants contain a hardening substance called *lignin* which makes them relatively rigid and inflexible; herbaceous plants contain little or no lignin in their cells and are comparatively easy to cut or break. Herbaceous stems are usually green; woody stems ordinarily lack the green coloring. When severe frost comes, herbaceous plants are killed and collapse on the ground while woody plants, due to their lignified cells, remain upright although they may lose their leaves.

In most cases it is not difficult to distinguish herbaceous plants from woody ones. However, there are borderline cases such as St. Andrew's Cross (*Ascyrum hypericoides*), see Fig. 106, and Swamp Loosestrife (*Decodon verticillatus*), see Fig. 135, which are somewhat woody. Some persons would call these shrubs, others might classify them as herbaceous plants. Vines, too, may vary. Trumpet-flower, Wild Grape, and Wisteria are woody vines whereas Climbing Fumitory (*Adlumia fungosa*) see Fig. 158, Groundnut (*Apios americana*) see Fig. 165, and Wild Balsamapple (*Echinocystis lobata*) see Fig. 275, are herbaceaus and clamber over other plants or trail along on the ground.

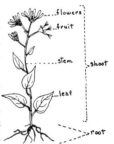

It is now clear that in this book we will be concerned with plants that produce flowers and seeds and in most cases have herbaceous stems. And as the title indicates, they will be plants found in bloom in the fall.

THE AVERAGE SEED-BEARING PLANT

Usually a seed-bearing plant has an underground root system and a shoot which is above ground. The shoot is generally made up of a stem which bears leaves and flowers. The flowers in turn produce fruit and seeds.

Of course, differences in environment may often make two plants of the same species appear quite unlike each other. Here is a Fringed Gentian that grew in poor soil, had inadequate moisture, and received insufficient sunlight. Plant diseases and insects attacked this already poor specimen and made it even more straggly and stunted. We would not call this miserable plant truly representative of the species nor would we designate as typical a "blue ribbon" Fringed Gentian which had received extra-ordinary attention to all its requirements. The typical or average plant of the species falls somewhere between these two extremes. It will be understood that mention of plant height, number of leaves, size of flowers, and so on will apply to an average plant of its kind.

PLANT PROCESSES

Are plants really important? To the person who does not care for the out-of-doors and who regards salads as "rabbit food", plants may seem rather insignificant. An indication of the vital role of the green plant will be found in the following important statement. OF ALL LIVING THINGS ONLY THE GREEN PLANT IS ABLE TO CAPTURE THE ENERGY OF SUNLIGHT AND STORE IT FOR FUTURE USE. This potential energy takes the form of food for the plant itself, food for all animals (including man), and fuels such as coal and oil. A prolonged strike by the green plants would mean extinction for all living things.

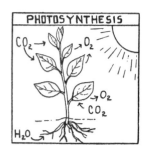

In this highly important chemical process the plant takes carbon dioxide (CO_2) from the air and water (H_2O) from the soil and in the presence of sunlight makes these simple compounds into complex organized foods called carbohydrates (plant sugars and starches). *Photosynthesis* is the name of this extremely vital chemical action. It takes place only in the presence of sunlight (or sometimes artificial light) and is carried on mainly in the green leaf (green because of *chlorophyll*). Oxygen O_2) is a by-product that is released into the air.

A few seed-bearing plants have either an insufficient supply of chlorophyll or none at all and thus cannot manufacture their own food. Beach-drops (*Epifagus virginiana*), see Fig. 211, is a yellowish-brown plant with no chlorophyll that gets its food from the roots of beech trees. It is called a *parasite* because its sustenance comes from a living plant. Coralroot (*Corallorhiza odontorhiza*), see Fig. 45, is a brownish-purple forest plant of the Orchid Family. Because it lives on dead vegetable matter it is called a *saprophyte*. Fortunately for us the majority of the world's plants continue to make their own food and thus supply man and all the other animals with the fuel for life.

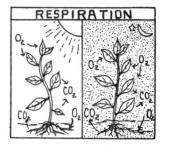

The first main function of any plant is development and maintenance of its own existence. Next is the reproduction of its kind. These activities take energy. In a manner similar to human respiration, the plant takes oxygen from the air to "burn" the food stored in its root, stem, or other parts and thus energy is released for all plant activities — growth, production of flowers, fruit, and seeds. This oxidation of stored food to release needed energy is

4

called *respiration* and as in human respiration carbon dioxide (CO_2) is liberated into the air. This process is going on continually throughout the 24 hours with all living plants.

Each plant has an intricate transportation system of "pipes" called *vascular bundles*. Through these bundles water and raw materials from the soil are carried to all parts of the plant and newly-manufactured food is transported to a storage place — such as root of carrot, head of cabbage, or shoot of asparagus. The large veins in a leaf are an evident part of this vascular system which branches and re-branches in order to serve all parts of the plant. The well-known strings within stalks of celery and those seen in banana fruit are part of the vascular system of those plants.

vascular bundles

Another plant activity is *transpiration* in which a plant may lose by evaporation from the leaves several hundred times its own weight in water. In experiments in transpiration, a sunflower plant lost over one pint of water a day, a corn plant about two quarts of water per day. Thus an extensive wooded area probably has a marked effect on the climate of the region due to the large amounts of moisture being transpired.

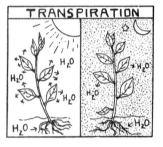

Naturally a very important plant activity is the production of seed so that the species will continue. One of the first steps in this process is *pollination*, which may be accomplished by the wind (as in the oaks, willows); water (the pondweeds and other aquatic plants); insects and other animals (the large majority of plants are pollinated in this way). Some plants are self-pollinated but many ingenious plant devices for preventing this make it the exception rather than the rule. Plants have many ways of attracting insects so that pollination will be assured. Odor and color followed up in each case by giving nectar, are the two most commonly employed.

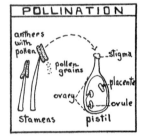

Various bees, wasps, flies and other insects while engaged in collecting nectar incidently carry pollen on their hairy bodies from the stamens of one plant to the stigma of another plant of the same species. Prolonged rainy weather in the spring often means a small strawberry and raspberry crop because the insects cannot get out to the flowers.

Normally many grains of pollen find their way to the stigma but only one grain is needed to fertilize each ovule. The ovules are fastened on projections (placentae) on the inside of the protecting ovary where they develop into mature seeds. The number of ovules and therefore the number of seeds varies in different species — from one to many and the number is not always constant in the same species. Our domestic honey bee and many species of wild bees collect pollen to feed their young. This requires the plants to increase the supply to insure adequate pollination.

THE LEAF

There is much variation in leaves as to margins, tips, bases, shape, etc. Many of these facts can be presented more clearly by illustrations than by descriptions. Use these drawings for reference at first and soon they will be automatically remembered. Fig. 1.

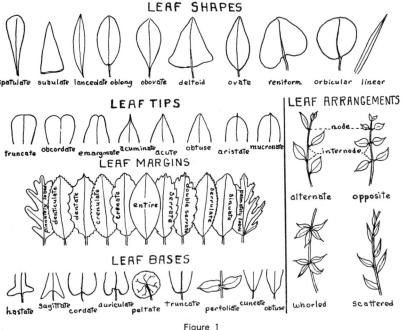

Figure 1

A simple leaf ordinarily consists of a flattened, expanded portion (blade) usually with a slender stalk (petiole) and often two, small leaf-like appendages (stipules) at the base of the petiole. Some leaves have no petioles and are said to be sessile. A compound leaf has several

6

to many *leaflets* and according to the arrangement of these leaflets is *pinnately* or *palmately compound*. A true leaf has a bud in its axil, a leaflet does not. A leaf may be *parallel-veined* or *net-veined*. Fig. 2.

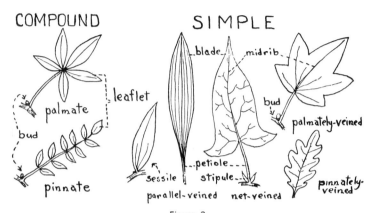

COMPOUND   SIMPLE

leaflet

palmate

bud

pinnate

blade   midrib

bud

palmately-veined

sessile   stipule

petiole

parallel-veined   net-veined

pinnately-veined

Figure 2

THE FLOWER

In most cases the flower is more often used as a means of indentifying the plant than are the leaves, stem, roots, etc. The floral parts of a species show much less variation from plant to plant and from

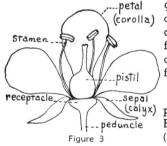

petal (corolla)

Stamen

pistil

receptacle

sepal (calyx)

peduncle

Figure 3

generation to generation than do the other plant structures. Therefore if we are to be on familiar terms with fall flowers it is quite essential that we refer often to these facts about the parts of a flower until they are well in mind.

A *complete flower* has four sets of parts, all of which are modified leaves. From the outside to the inside they are: (1) a *calyx* composed of *sepals*, (2) a *corolla* composed of *petals*, (3) *stamens* that may be separate or united, (4) a *pistil* of one to many *carpels*. These floral parts are arranged on the broadened tip *(receptacle)* of the flower stalk *(peduncle)*. Fig. 3. However, only the main stalk of a single flower or of a group of flowers is the peduncle; the stalk of each individual flower of a group is a *pedicel*. Fig. 4.

pedicel

peduncle

Figure 4

7

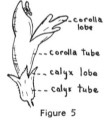

Figure 5

In some flowers the sepals are united into a tube or the petals make a tubular or bell-shaped corolla. Fig. 5. When only one set of the floral envelopes (sepals and petals) is present, we arbitrarily call it the calyx. The calyx and corolla together are known as the *perianth*.

Figure 6

A *perfect flower* has both stamens and pistils with or without sepals and petals. The stamens and pistils are often called the *essential parts* because they are the only structures that actually function to produce seed. Fig. 6.

Figure 7

A stamen consists of a pollen-bearing *anther* which is usually supported by a slender stalk (*filament*). Fig. 7.

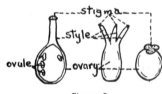

Figure 8

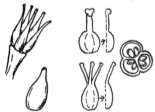

Simple pistils of one carpel   Compound pistils of three carpels

Figure 9

A pistil (Fig. 8) always has an ovary and *stigma*. A stem-like *style* often separates these two parts. The enlarged basal ovary contains *ovules* which ripen into seeds after fertilization. The stigma is the tip that receives the pollen; it is connected to the ovary by the style which varies in length and may even be absent. Sometimes there are several stigmas, each with its own style. Fig. 8. A *carpel* is a simple pistil or one section of a compound pistil. Fig. 9.

staminate   pistillate

Figure 10

A flower may have stamens only (*staminate*) or pistils only (*pistillate* or *carpellate*). Fig. 10. A *dioecious* plant is one that has either all staminate (male) or all pistillate (female) flowers. A *monoecious* plant bears both staminate and pistillate flowers.

Flowers are *solitary* or *clustered*. The method of arrangement of the flowers is called the *inflorescence*. Fig. 11 shows the most common inflorescence types.

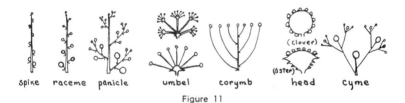

spike   raceme   panicle   umbel   corymb   head   cyme

Figure 11

FLOWERS OF THE COMPOSITAE

A study of fall flowers brings us in close contact with many of the Compositae or Daisy Family. The flowers of this highly specialized group are somewhat different from flowers of other families so we will devote extra attention to them at this point.

In the Compositae (asters, sunflowers, goldenrods, daisies, etc.) what is commonly thought of as one flower is in reality many small flowers crowded together on a common receptacle. The entire head is subtended by an involucre of several to many bracts which are usually leaf-like.

These tiny flowers are of two kinds: *disk flowers* (also called *tube flowers*) and *ray flowers* (also called *ligulate flowers*). The disk flowers which make up the central part of the head have tubular corollas, while the ray flowers which are usually around the edge of the head have strap-shaped corollas and are commonly (and erroneously) called petals. Quite often these ray flowers are sterile, with only the disk flowers producing seed. A head may be composed of disk flowers or ray flowers only, or both. Thistles and burdock have disk flowers only, chicory and dandelion have ray flowers only, sunflowers have both ray and disk flowers.

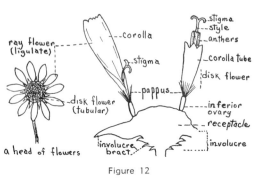

Figure 12

In practically all cases, each of these small flowers consist of (1) a pistil with an inferior ovary, a single style, and a two-parted stigma, (2) five stamens with the anthers united into a tube which surrounds the style, (3) a corolla of 5 petals (either tube-shaped or strap-shaped), (4) a calyx reduced to a ring of tissue, scales, bristles, or teeth (or sometimes absent) and collectively called the *pappus*. Fig. 12.

FRUIT AND SEEDS

Fruit, in the popular sense, means apples, cherries, strawberries, raspberries, oranges, etc. In the botanical sense, fruits also include walnuts, *grain* or corn, wheat, rice and other grasses, *samara* of maple, pod of bean, and other less-familiar fruits.

The mature ovary with its one to many seeds is the *fruit*. There are a few plant species in which the ovary wall will develop into a seedless fruit if the ovules are not fertilized. Examples of this are banana, pineapple, seedless raisin grape, and navel orange. Usually, however, the ovary will not develop unless at least some of the ovules are fertilized.

Fruits are *fleshy* or *dry*. Fleshy fruits include the *berry* of the Tomato family — Solanaceae, *pepo* of the Cucumber family — Cucurbitaceae.

Dry fruits are *dehiscent* (opening to discharge the seeds) or *indehiscent* (do not open to discharge the seed). Dehiscent fruits include pod (or legume) of the Bean family, milkweed *follicle,* mustard *silique,* capsule of Lily family.

Some indehiscent fruits are *achene* of Buttercup and Compositae family, *utricle* of Chenepodiaceae, Amaranthaceae, *nutlets* of Mint, Vervain, Borage family, *loment* of Lespedeza, Desmodium, schizocarp of Carrot family. Fig. 13.

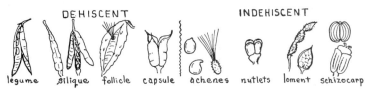

Figure 13

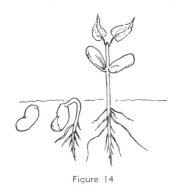

Figure 14

The *seed* is a partially-developed young plant with embryonic root, stem and leaves, plus an ample food supply. This embryo plant is well-protected by the hard outer *seed-coat* and may remain dormant for many months before circumstances favorable to growth are present. During germination, the growing plant uses its stored food reserves until it has developed green leaves and can then manufacture food for itself. Seed dispersal is accomplished mainly by wind, water, and animals (man included). Fig. 14.

NAMES

Lobelia cardinalis L. is the scientific name of a red-flowered plant belonging to the Lobelia Family. Several of its common names are: Red Lobelia, Cardinal Flower, Slink Weed, Red Betty. Obviously, it saves time and misunderstanding to use the one scientific name of a plant, rather than attempting to remember the numerous common names it usually has. And scientific names are the same the world over, regardless of country or language.

All scientific names are in Latin. In the above case, *Lobelia* is the *generic* name, *cardinalis* the species name. Names of the genus are always capitalized. The species names of animals always begin with small letters. Although some botanists use capital letters for some species names, we prefer to begin all the species names with small letters. Scientific names are underscored or printed in italic type.

The word or abbreviation following the genus and species names stands for the scientist who proposed the name and is known as the "Author" or "Authority". A good many of our animals and plants, including *Lobelia cardinalis* L. were named by Linnaeus, a famous Swedish naturalist, who devised the Binomial (meaning two names) System of plant and animal nomenclature. This Binomial System has been in use since around 1750.

For the most part, the classification and scientific names used in this book are the same as in Gray's Manual. Many sources have been consulted for the most widely-used common name of each plant.

SOME SUGGESTIONS ABOUT A HERBARIUM

lmost everyone has at some time pressed a flower or leaf between the pages of a book. This is fine for sentimental reasons, but hard on the book. For a note-worthy *herbarium* (a collection of plants carefully pressed and dried, and accurately mounted and labeled) more desirable methods than haphazard book-pressing are suggested.

What better way to record your vacations or your travels than by gathering representative plants on these occasions. Or make a collection of a particular family, genus, or other group of plants of your region. Even the vacant city lot yields a surprising number of different plant species. You will spend many absorbing hours working your plants into a herbarium that will give you keen satisfaction.

The main steps for making a herbarium are: (for more complete instructions see How to Know the Spring Flowers.)

1. *Collecting.* Select plants in good condition that are representative of their species. Protect them from heat and wind by carrying them in a container such as a box or a paper sack. Persons

who really enjoy the out-of-doors will not pick or uproot plants in a wholesale manner. For most herbariums it is quite unnecessary to have the roots. Sometimes just a few leaves and flowers are sufficient. If it's a weed collection you're making, help yourself to the entire plant. No one would object if you pulled a few extra of these.

2. *Pressing and Drying.* Place each plant, along with the date and place of collection, in a *folder* (one thickness of absorbent newspaper folded once is good). Alternate the folders with the *dryers*, which may also be made of newspaper but of 16 to 20 thicknesses. A heavy weight placed on a board (to distribute the pressure) is now put on top of the entire stack of folders and dryers.

The dryers, which absorb moisture from the plants, need to be changed often (once or twice a day) and dry ones substituted. On the average it will take about a week to complete the pressing and drying process. All this time the plants remain in the original folders.

3. *Mounting.* By means of glue or transparent tape, fasten the dry plant to a sheet of paper. In the lower right hand corner affix a label bearing the following data: scientific, common, and family names, date and place collected, habitat, and collector. If this information is inaccurate or missing, your herbarium is practically worthless from the scientific standpoint.

4. *Arrangement.* Arrange the species in the order they appear in a plant manual (such as Gray's Manual). If your herbarium is carefully handled, kept dry, and protected from insects (paradichlorobenzene crystals are excellent) it should remain in good condition indefinitely.

SOME HELPFUL REFERENCE BOOKS

umerous books have been written about plants, seemingly from nearly every angle. The following list includes some of the best of their type, but is not intended to be all-inclusive.

"Gray's Manual of Botany"—8th edition—M. L. Fernald

"Illustrated Flora of the Northern United States and Canada"—Britton and Brown

"Manual of the Southeastern Flora"—John K. Small

"Flora of the Prairies and Plains of Central North America"—P. A. Rydberg

"Field Manual of the Flora of Ohio"—John H. Schaffner

"Wild Flowers of Ohio"—H. L. Madison

"Fieldbook of Illinois Wild Flowers"—Illinois Natural History Survey

"Flora of Illinois"—George Neville Jones

"Pioneering with Wildflowers"—George D. Aiken

"Aquatic Plants of the United States"—Walter C. Muenscher

"Plants of Iowa"—Henry S. Conard

"Wild Flowers of Louisiana"—Caroline Dormon

"Southern Wild Flowers and Trees"—Alice Lounsberry

"Plant Families"—H. E. Jaques

"A Guide to the Wild Flowers"—Norman Taylor

"Field Book of American Wild Flowers"—F. Schuyler Mathews

"Wild Flowers"—Homer D. House

"Our Wild Orchids"—Morris and Eames

"Our Northern Autumn Flowers"—H. L. Keeler

"Guide to Wild Flowers"—Arthur Craig Quick

"Flora of Indiana"—Charles C. Deam

"Wild Flower Guide"—Edgar T. Wherry

HOW TO USE THE KEYS

Usually the quickest and most accurate way of finding the name of a flower is by use of keys. With your unknown plant at hand, you consider two (rarely 3) statements — one true of the flower in question, the other untrue. By accurate choice of the correct statements, you come to the name of your flower.

To illustrate: You are hiking along a lake and come across a patch of blue flowers growing in the water. You have your copy of "Fall Flowers" with you, so out it comes and you turn to page 16 and start to key this plant. Comparing 1a with 1b your plant has parallel-veined leaves and a blue perianth of 6 parts so it is a Monocotyledon and you go to 2. Statement 2b is the correct one as sepals and petals are both present although they are similar. There is but one pistil so 4b is the proper choice here. You go on to 8. Comparing statement 8a with 8b it is quite clear that 8a is correct because your plant has a superior ovary instead of an inferior one. This takes you to 9a and 9b, where 9b is the true statement and you go on to consider 13a and 13b. There is no doubt whether this plant is aquatic or terrestrial so it's on to 14 where 14a is right because of the 2-lipped blue perianth and 6 stamens. It's Pickerel-weed (*Pontederia cordata* L.). You read the description, compare the growing plant with the illustration, and feel sure that you have keyed your plant to its correct name. Being an enthusiastic fisherman you wonder if there is any connection between the name Pickerel-weed and the fish of the name pickerel. The description doesn't say but you have the name of your plant and can look it up elsewhere for this or any further information you desire.

Sometimes two plants seem very similar when reading their descriptions. Perhaps in comparing them the first has softer and more abundant pubescence, the leaves are a trifle more narrow, the flowers a little darker yellow. In such a case, there is no big outstanding difference between the two, but several small, scarcely noticeable differences. However, carefuly observe these plants and you will soon recognize them without doubt, each time you see them. You may not be able to tell why you know them, except that they simply look right. Just as we all know two persons who look much alike — weight and height about the same, eye and hair color very similar, features of the same general type — yet we always greet them with their correct names.

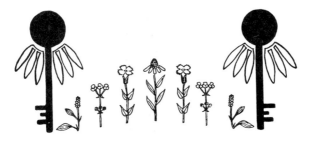

15

PICTURED-KEYS FOR IDENTIFYING THE MORE COMMON FALL-FLOWERING HERBACEOUS PLANTS

1a Leaves usually parallel-veined (a); flowering parts usually in 3's (b); stem hollow or with scattered vascular bundles (c); seed usually with one cotyledon. Fig. 15.
MONOCOTYLEDONS 2

Figure 15

1b Leaves usually net-veined (a); parts of the flower mostly in 4's or 5's (b); stem with a ring of vascular bundles surrounding the pith (c); seed usually with two cotyledons. Fig. 16.
DICOTYLEDONS ....page 30

Figure 16

MONOCOTYLEDONS

2a Perianth (sepals and petals) of bristles or wanting (the anthers of *Potamogeton* (Fig. 18a) have appendages which might be mistaken for sepals). 3

2b Flowers with sepals and petals (sometimes the two are very similar). Fig. 17. 4

Figure 17

3a Submerged aquatics, usually with some of the leaves floating; perianth none. Fig. 18.
LARGE-LEAVED PONDWEED *Potamogeton amplifolius* Tuckerm.

This largest and coarsest of the pondweeds has two types of thin submerged leaves. The long lanceolate lower ones are usually folded lengthwise and curved sickle-fashion; the broader upper ones are 2½ to 7 inches long. Usually leathery floating leaves are present.

As in all of the pondweeds, the spikes are raised on a stem to the water's surface where the flowers are fertilized by floating pollen grains.

Figure 18

16

3b Plant not normally submerged although growing in wet places; flowers in dense cylindric spikes; perianth of bristles. Fig. 19a.
                              BROAD-LEAVED CAT-TAIL *Typha latifolia* L.

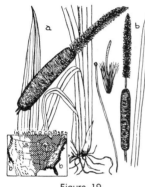

This stout perennial (3-6 ft. high) of marshes, swamps and ditches grows in temperate regions throughout the entire world often covering hundreds of acres. The light brown staminate flowers at the top of the spike are usually touching the lower dark brown pistillate-flowered area.

NARROW-LEAVED CAT-TAIL *Typha angustifolia* L. Fig. 19b grows scattered throughout North America but is more common near the coast. The cat-tails bloom (shed pollen) in late spring but are conspicuous during the summer and fall.

Figure 19

4a Carpels several to many, distinct (in *Triglochin* the carpels are united until maturity). Fig. 20. 5

Figure 20

4b Carpels united into one compound pistil. Fig. 21. 8

Figure 21

5a Petals and sepals similar. Fig. 22.
                        SEASIDE ARROW GRASS *Triglochin maritima* L.

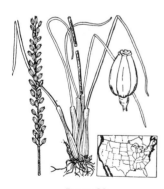

A stout narrow-leaved plant (8 to 20 inches high) usually found in salt marshes in the east and fresh water westward. The small whitish blossoms are borne in long terminal racemes which are often over 12 inches in length. The flower has 6 perianth segments, each with a large anther. The pistil has 6 united carpels which separate at maturity. Also found in Europe and Asia.

Two similar species are *Triglochin palustris* L. of northern areas and southerly *Triglochin striata* R. & P. Both plants prefer a marshy habitat.

Figure 22

5b Sepals herbaceous, persistent; petals delicate, white or pinkish, deciduous (falling off). 6

6a Carpels (simple pistils) in a ring (a); flowers perfect (with both pistils and stamens); stamens usually 6. Fig. 23.

WATER PLANTAIN *Alisma subcordatum* Raf.

A rather inconspicuous plant (8 to 20 inches high) of swamps, ditches and shallow water bearing long-petioled oval leaves and one of two loose compound panicles of small white-petaled flowers. Each flower has 3 persistent sepals, 3 deciduous petals with 2 stamens opposite each one, and a ring of many pistils on the flat receptacle.

This plant belongs in the Alismaceae family as do also the closely related Arrow-heads of the genus *Sagittaria*.

Figure 23

6b Carpels in a dense head (See Fig. 25a); plants monoecious (with both staminate and pistillate flowers) or dioecious (bearing only staminate or only pistillate flowers); stamens mostly numerous....7

7a Leaves usually broad with sagittate bases; flower 1 to 1½ inches broad; achene with a long beak (a). Fig. 24.

BROAD-LEAVED ARROW-HEAD *Sagittaria latifolia* Willd.

Almost everyone has seen this common and attractive plant (8 to 24 inches high) which grows in swamps, along river-banks, and in shallow water.

The large showy flowers have 3 persistent sepals, 3 white deciduous petals and either many pistils in a dense head or numerous stamens. The lower flowers are pistillate the upper staminate. The fruiting heads (⅜ to one inch broad) consist of many long-beaked achenes.

Figure 24

18

7b Leaves usually linear to lanceolate, rarely with sagittate bases; flower 1/3 to ½ inch broad; achene almost beakless (b). Fig. 25.

GRASS-LEAVED SAGITTARIA *Sagittaria graminea* Michx.

Figure 25

This plant grows in mud and shallow water to a height of ½ to 2 feet. The leaves have narrow, linear blades on long petioles and are less "grass-like" than several other species. The greenish-white flowers with 15 to 18 stamens have a breadth of ½ inch or less. The achenes are without a beak or with only a minute one.

The genus name refers to the leafblades of some species which are shaped like an arrow-head, but this and several other species do not have such leafblades at all. CRESTED SAGITTARIA *S. cristata* Engelm., growing in shallow water in Minn. and Iowa and EATON'S SAGITTARIA *S. eatoni* Smith, a marine form growing in sandy places along the Atlantic Coast both have narrow grass-like leaves.

8a Ovary superior (hypogynous—above the calyx). Fig. 26. 9

Figure 26

8b Ovary partly or wholly inferior (epigynous—below the calyx). Fig. 27. 19

Figure 27

9a Flowers crowded in small dense terminal scaly heads (usually less than one inch long); inflorescence with chaffy bracts among the tiny flowers. 10

9b Flowers variously arranged but not in small dense scaly heads; no chaffy bracts present among the flowers. 13

10a Flowers perfect (with both stamens and pistils), in oval scaly spikes; corolla yellow. 11

10b Flowers usually monoecious (with either stamens or pistils, but not both in the same flower) in gray or white woolly heads. 12

11a Leaves and scapes usually spirally twisted; plant base dark, bulbous-thickened; lateral sepals ¼ to ½ inch long, the wing fringed and bearded. Fig. 28a.

SLENDER YELLOW-EYED GRASS *Xyris flexuosa* Muhl.

Figure 28

A grass-like plant (10 to 24 inches high) of acid swamps and pinelands with a dark bulbous base, spirally-twisted linear leaves, and naked scapes bearing small flowers in oblong spikes (about one inch long). Each flower consists of 3 sepals (one falling away), 3 yellow petals, 3 fertile stamens alternating with 3 sterile bearded ones, and a pistil with a 3-cleft style.

TWISTED YELLOW-EYED GRASS *X. fimbriata* Ell., Fig. 28b, has its lateral sepals winged instead of wingless as in *flexuosa*. It grows along the coast in wet pine barrens from New Jersey to Florida and west to Mississippi. It stands 2 to 4 feet high.

11b Leaves and scapes mostly straight; plant base not thickened; lateral sepals ⅛ inch long, the wing toothed above the middle (a). Fig. 29.

CAROLINA YELLOW-EYED GRASS *Xyris caroliniana* Walt.

Figure 29

This plant grows in swamps and bogs and attains a height of 1 to 2 feet. The leaves are less than a half inch wide but may attain a length up to 15 inches. The flowers are yellow.

TALL YELLOW-EYED GRASS *X. smalliana* Nash, attaining a height of 4 feet or more has more elongate heads. It is found in low pinelands and coastal swamps from Virginia to Florida and Louisiana.

12a Leaf blades longer than the sheaths (a); scapes 10 to 14 angled; heads 1/3 to 2/3 inch broad. Fig. 30.

TEN-ANGLED PIPEWORT *Eriocaulon decangulare* **L.**

Figure 30

This swamp-growing plant attains a height of 1 to 3 feet. The leaves are around ½ inch wide and ½ to 1½ feet long. The tiny whitish, woolly flowers are crowded in a globular head which is supported on a long sturdy scape. The plant gets its name from the 10 to 16 ridges on this scape.

12b Leaf blades shorter than the sheaths; scapes 4 to 8 angled; heads less than ¼ inch broad. Fig. 31.

SEVEN-ANGLED PIPEWORT *Eriocaulon septangulare* **With.**

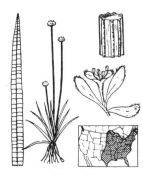

Figure 31

A rather inconspicuous but common plant of wet sandy places often submerged in water and then usually taller than its average one to 8 inches. The soft basal leaves are awl-shaped. The usually 7-grooved slender scapes terminate in whitish woolly heads which bear the tiny flowers. Another common name is Hatpins, a delightfully appropriate one.

14a Flowers many; perianth blue, 2-lipped; stamens 6. Fig. 32.

PICKEREL-WEED *Pontederia cordata* L.

Figure 32

A beautiful aquatic plant (one to 4 feet tall) often growing in masses in lakes, marshes and streams. The thick root-leaves are long-petioled, many nerved; the single stem-leaf is similar except for its short petiole. The stout spike bears many violet-blue ephemeral flowers.

The funnel-form perianth is marked on its upper middle lobe with a pair of yellow spots. There are 3 long-exserted stamens and 3 often sterile or imperfect ones with short filaments and all six usually bright blue. The 3-celled ovary has 2 empty cavities; the bladder-like fruit is one-seeded.

14b Flowers few; perianth yellow, regular; stamens 3. Fig. 33.

WATER STAR-GRASS *Heteranthera dubia* (Jacq.)

Figure 33

This plant is widely distributed in quiet waters; the slender stems have a length of 2 to 3 feet and often take root at the nodes. The pale yellow flowers are ½ inch or more across. The three-celled capsule bears many seeds.

Other species of the genus have broad leafblades and are known as mud-plantains.

15a Perianth of 3 persistent green sepals and 3 ephemeral (lasting but a day) mostly blue petals; stamens 6, usually sterile. 16

15b Perianth of 6 very similar divisions; stamens 6, all fertile. 17

16a Spathe-like involucre (a) not united at the base; 2 lateral petals blue, anterior petal smaller, white. Fig. 34.

ASIATIC DAY-FLOWER *Commelina communis* L.

Figure 34

This slender decumbent Asiatic native is now a familiar sight in dooryards, gardens and waste places. It is one to 3 feet long with dark green leaves and irregular flowers (½ inch wide) subtended in spathe-like bracts. The two lateral petals are deep blue and have claws; the anterior petal is smaller and white. The flowers last but a day.

16b Spathe-like involucre united at the base; all 3 petals blue. Fig. 35.

VIRGINIA DAY-FLOWER *Commelina virginica* L.

Figure 35

The stems of this branching plant are somewhat spreading and attain a length of 1 to 3 feet. The linear-lanceolate leaves are up to 5 inches in length with inflated sheathes. The bright blue flowers are about an inch across and showy. The capsule has 3 cells with 1 seed in each cell. It grows best in moist soil and is frequently planted as an ornamental.

17a Plant with a mild onion-like odor; flowers pinkish, in umbels. Fig. 36.

PRAIRIE WILD ONION *Allium stellatum* Ker.

Figure 36

This plant has many slender flat leaves and attains a height of 8 to 16 inches. The numerous pink flowers are borne in an erect umbel. The style and stamens are excerted. The onion odor is less pronounced than in many related species. It grows on rocky banks and sandy prairies.

17b Plant not alliaceous (with an onion-like odor); flowers yellowish or greenish-white, in panicles (the persistent perianth of *Melanthium* often turns reddish-brown). 18

18a Sepals and petals with 2 glands at the base of each blade (a); panicle branches pubescent. Fig. 37.

BUNCH-FLOWER *Melanthium virginicum* L.

Figure 37

This sturdy perennial attains a height of 2 to 5 feet; the linear grass-like leaves may be nearly an inch in width and a foot long. The greenish-yellow flowers, ½ inch or more across, presently turn brown; they are numerous in a large panicle. Each petal bears 2 conspicuous glands near its base. Several seeds are borne in each of the 3 cavities of the inch or longer capsule.

18b Sepals and petals glandless; panicle branches glabrous (without hairs or roughness). Fig. 38.

GRASS-LEAVED STENANTHIUM *Stenanthium gramineum* (Ker.)

Figure 38

This plant is somewhat like the preceding to which it is related. It has a height of 3 to 4 feet but is more slender and the leaves are narrower. The numerous whitish flowers are borne in a panicle 1 to 2 feet long; the perianth segments are narrow and sharp pointed; they have no glands. It grows in dry soil, often in the mountains.

19a Submerged aquatic plant; flowers dioecious. Fig. 39.

TAPE GRASS *Vallisneria americana* Michx.

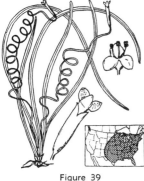

Figure 39

A common plant of ponds and streams with long ribbon-like leaves. The numerous stamens are crowded on a spadix which breaks from its short stalk and floats to the water's surface there to shed pollen on the pistillate flowers that have been raised to the air on long slender scapes. Afterwards the scapes coil up spirally and pull the fruit under water to ripen. Often called Water-celery. It is a favorite food of wild ducks.

19b Land plants (sometimes of marshy places but never normally submerged); flowers perfect. 20

20a Flowers regular (Fig. 40); fertile stamens 3 or 6. 21

Figure 40

20b Flowers irregular (Fig. 41); fertile stamen one. 22

Figure 41

21a Flowers white, large (over 5 inches long); stamens 6. Fig. 42.

HYMENOCALLIS *Hymenocallis occidentalis* (Le Conte)

Figure 42

This is one of some 40 species of "Spider Lilies", all American and several native of our South. They grow from a large bulb. This species has a height of 1 to 2 feet. The usually 6 flowers are borne in an umbel and have a conspicuous crown as pictured. The flowers are white with bright yellow anthers and are very fragrant. A green capsule bears 1 or 2 large fleshy green seeds.

25

21b Flowers yellowish, hairy, small (½ inch long or less); stamens 3.
Fig. 43.   RED-ROOT *Lachnanthes tinctoria* (Walt.)

Figure 43

Growing to a height of 2 feet or more, this plant has acquired its name from its fibrous red roots. The spreading panicle contains several rather small yellow flowers. The fruit is a small globular capsule. It is found in swamps. Another name is Spirit-weed.

22a Yellowish or purplish saprophytes; leaves reduced to scales...23

22b Plants green; leaves not scale-like (in *Spiranthes* the leaves are sometimes absent or inconspicuous at flowering time). 24

23a Lip deeply 3-lobed (a), ¼ inch or more in length; capsules (seed pod) ⅜ to ¾ inch long. Fig. 44.
            LARGE CORAL-ROOT *Corallorhiza maculata* Raf.

Figure 44

This very interesting Orchid is at its best on wooded upland slopes, where it may reach a height of 1½ feet. Its 10 to 40 flowers are borne in a loose raceme and are about ¾ inch in length. The ground color of the flowers is white; they are beautifully ornamented with spots and streaks of purple, pink, brown and yellow. The genus gets its name from the coral-shaped root-stalk. Some 15 species are known but this is the largest one.

26

23b Lip not 3-lobed, but with wavy-crinkled margins (a), less than ¼ inch long; capsules about ¼ inch long. Fig. 45.

LATE CORAL ROOT *Corallorhiza odontorhiza* (Willd.)

The slender purplish scape has a height of 6 to 15 inches and bears 5 to 20 flowers which are white and strongly marked with purple. The members of this genus are saprophytes or root parasites so have only scale like leaves and no chlorophyll. This species grows in woods and is smaller than most of the other species.

Figure 45

24a Flowers with a conspicuous slender spur about ⅜ inch long (a). Fig. 46.

SOUTHERN SMALL WHITE ORCHIS *Habenaria nivea* (Nutt.)

This plant with grass-like leaves and slender stem has a height of 10 to 14 inches. The numerous small white or pinkish flowers grow in a spike some 4 inches long. It grows in low pine barrens. Other names are White Rein-orchid and Frog-spear. The flowers have an unusually long spur.

Figure 46

24b Flowers without a spur. 25
25a Flowers several, nodding, axillary, pinkish, ½ to 2/3 inch long. Fig. 47. NODDING POGONIA *Triphora trianthophora* (Sw.)

This little tuberous-rooted plant has a height of 3 to 8 inches. The 2 to several alternate leaves are ovate and less than an inch long. The 3 white to pink flowers have given it the name Three Birds.

Orchids on the whole, thrive best in the tropics, many of them being epiphytes. Some ten thousand species are known, world wide but less than 200 have been recorded for the United States and Canada.

Figure 47

25b Flowers usually many in a terminal spike, mostly white or cream-color, usually less than ½ inch long. 26

26a Leaves with a network of white markings; lip pouch-like at base (a). Fig. 48.
DOWNY RATTLESNAKE PLANTAIN *Goodyera pubescens* (Willd.)

The glandular-pubescent scape may reach a height of 20 inches and bears several small greenish-white flowers. It grows in dry evergreen woods; a rosette of 1 to 2 inch bluish-green leaves netted with whitish veins is at the base while the scape bears several slender leaves. The lip is inflated and the whole flower more compactly rounded than is usual with orchids.

Figure 48

26b Leaves entirely green (occasionally absent at flowering time); lip not pouch-like, but with a horn-like callosity (hardened thickening) within on each side at the base. (Fig. 49a). 27

Figure 49

27a Flowers, by twisting of the main flower stem, in a single spiral, often onesided. 28

27b Flowers in 2 or 3 spirals. 29

28a Leaves linear, 2½ to 6 inches long, mostly persistent; stem leafy, usually very pubescent above; flowers yellowish. Fig. 50.
LINEAR-LEAVED LADIES'-TRESSES *Spiranthes vernalis*
Engelm. & Gray.

This slender stemmed plant is rather widely distributed in both wet and dry soils and has a height of 6 to 20 inches. The grass-like leaves are 3 to 6 inches long. The numerous small yellowish flowers are arranged in a spiral for 4 to 6 inches at the top of the spike. The lower part of the scape is leafy.

Figure 50

28b Leaves ovate-lanceolate, ⅝ to 2 inches long, disappearing before flowering time; stem scaly, usually glabrous above; flowers white with a green stripe on the lip. Fig. 51.

SLENDER LADIES'-TRESSES *Spiranthes gracilis* (Bigel.)

Figure 51

This species grows in somewhat acid soil and has a height of 8 to 30 inches. The spike is very much twisted and bears numerous small white and green flowers. The few basal leaves are ovate and short petioled; they may measure 2 inches in length.

29a Sepals and petals more or less united and formed into a hood; lip constricted near the middle (a). Fig. 52.

HOODED LADIES'-TRESSES *Spiranthes romanzoffiana* Cham.

Figure 52

This most widely distributed of the ladies'-tresses grows to a height of 10 to 15 inches. The stem bears clasping grass-like leaves. The small flowers are borne spirally in three ranks in the spike.

Many of the orchids have peculiar schemes to insure cross fertilization; Darwin was the first to call attention to the ladies'-tresses. The flowers at the bottom of the spike mature earliest and the bees begin there and work up the spike. When the bee visits a flower the beak splits and a packet of fresh pollen is pasted to the bee's forehead from which it reaches the stigma of the next plant the bee visits.

29b Lateral sepals free and separate; lip not constricted or rarely slightly so. 30

30a Perianth over ¼ inch long; leaves linear, 2 to 14 inches long; flower spike thick, stout. Fig. 53.

NODDING LADIES'-TRESSES *Spiranthes cernua* (L.)

Growing in wet meadows and bogs, this species may attain a height of 2, feet though it is often much smaller. The flowers are pure white, highly fragrant and larger than the individual flowers of other members of the genus. The basal leaves often measuring a foot in length die before the flowers appear.

Figure 53

30b Perianth about 1/6 inch long; leaves broadly linear to linear-oblong, 1½ to 6½ inches long; flower spike slender. Fig. 54.

SMALL-FLOWERED LADIES'-TRESSES *Spiranthes ovalis* Lindl.

This species grows to a height of 5 to 15 inches and is found in woods and swamps. The leaves have a length of 2 to 6 inches. The small white flowers compactly fill the comparatively short spike. The lip is ovate and definitely narrowing towards its apex.

Our native orchids usually are quite restricted in their habitat requirements and need to be carefully protected.

Figure 54

DICOTYLEDONS

1a (a, b, c) Corolla (petals) none; calyx (sepals) present or absent, sometimes colored and resembling a corolla. Fig. 55. (*Penthorum* with petals wanting or inconspicuous, *Paronychia* with minute bristles representing petals). 2

Figure 55

1b Both calyx and corolla present. Fig. 56.
(Examine the buds because a few flowers
drop their sepals as soon as the flower
opens.) (Sepals obsolete (undeveloped) in
Conioselinum and *Ptilimnium*). 29

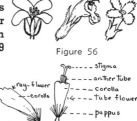

Figure 56

1c Flowers of one or more kinds crowded
in a head on a common receptacle
with one or more rings of bracts beneath; calyx or corolla rarely absent;
petals united; the 5 stamens usually
united to form a tube; ovary inferior;
one-celled, one-seeded.
Fig. 57 . . Compositae Family . page 112

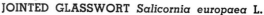

Figure 57

2a Aquatic plant resembling a seaweed,
attached to rocks in running water;
leaf-blades divided into many thread-
like linear segments. Fig. 58.
RIVER-WEED *Podostemum ceratophyllum*
Michx.

This rather stiff, dark green aquatic plant
attains a length of 4 to 10 inches. The solitary green flowers have two stamens; the
ovary is 2-celled and forms a capsule of 2
valves, one of which is persistent.

P. abrotanoides Nutt., ranging through the
southeastern states is a similar but larger
plant.

Figure 58

2b Land plants, although often in wet places but not submerged;
leaves (when present) simple or compound, not divided into narrow segments. 3

3a Without leaves; stems jointed, fleshy; green plant of salt-marshes
turning red in autumn. Fig. 59.

JOINTED GLASSWORT *Salicornia europaea* L.

An odd and interesting fleshy, jointed,
much-branched plant (6-18 inches high)
with small scale-like leaves and tiny
flowers sunk in the axils of the upper
scales. The plant turns a brilliant red in
autumn thus making colorful patches in
the salt-marshes where it is chiefly found.
Saline places of the interior are also its
habitat.

Most interesting of all, this plant occasionally grows in the run-off from pickle
factories. Salty to the taste, as are most
salt-marsh plants. Other descriptive common names are Saltwort, Pickle-plant, and
Samphire.

Figure 59

3b Leaves present. 4

4a Leaves compound with numerous leaflets,
or leaves deeply divided into 3 to 7 segments. Fig. 60. 5

Figure 60

4b Leaves simple, entire or toothed. Fig. 61. 7

Figure 61

5a Leaves 2 or 3 times compound; leaflets roundish to oblong; flowers
many in a large showy panicle (8-14 inches long). Fig. 62.
TALL MEADOW-RUE *Thalictrum polygamum* Muhl.

Figure 62

This sturdy, much-branched plant is
found in swamps and low open ground
and grows to a height of 3 to 10 feet. The
polygamous flowers may be either white
or purplish with filaments broadened at
their middle, and are borne in large panicles. Feather-columbine is another common name.

5b Leaves once-divided; leaflets mostly ovate to lanceolate; flowers
axillary or in spikes. 6

6a Leaves pinnately compound; flowers white, in dense terminal
showy spikes one to 6 inches long. Fig. 63.
CANADIAN BURNET *Sanguisorba canadensis* L.

Figure 63

This plant belongs in swamps and low
wet places; it is a perennial and grows to
a height of 1 to 6 feet. The compound
leaves have 7 to 15 leaflets and are often
well over a foot in length. The white or
greenish-white flowers have 4 long white
stamens which give the long dense spikes
a furry appearance.

S. officinalis L., a native of Europe and
having lavender flowers, is occasionally
found in our country.

6b Leaves deeply palmately divided; flowers greenish, axillary, dioecious (staminate flowers on one plant, pistillate on another). Fig. 64.
HEMP *Cannabis sativa* **L.**

Figure 64

A rather attractive coarse hairy plant (3-9 feet tall) with thin leaves and inconspicuous greenish flowers. The staminate flowers each with 5 sepals and 5 drooping stamens grow on one plant. On another plant we find the pistillate flowers each consisting of a thin entire calyx enveloping the pistil.

This Hasheesh or Marijuana plant has been introduced from Asia where it is grown for its tough stem fibers which are a substitute for flax. Hemp is also cultivated in this•country but is found mostly in waste places as an escape. The achene is used in bird seed and for poultry feed.

7a Flowers usually perfect (both stamens and pistils in same flower). Fig. 65. .... **8**

Figure 65

7b Flowers monoecious (staminate and pistillate flowers on same plant) or dioecious (staminate flowers on one plant, pistillate on another) or polygamous (with both perfect and imperfect flowers (with stamens or pistils only). **16**

8a Stipules (leaf-like appendages in leaf-axils) present (in Polygonaceae in the form of sheaths). Fig. 66a. **10**

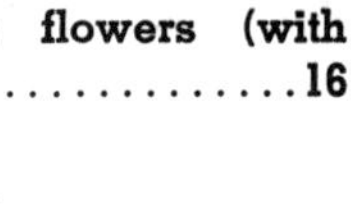

Figure 66

8b Plants without stipules. **9**

9a Leaves linear; pistil one, styles 2; fruit a one-seed utricle (bladdery one-seeded fruit). Fig. 67.

RUSSIAN THISTLE *Salsola kali tenuifolia* G. F. W. Mey.

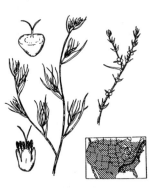

Figure 67

Originally from Asia, this bushy-branched plant has become an abundant and pernicious weed in sandy waste places—especially in the Central and Northwest States. The inconspicuous sessile flowers are axillary. The linear prickle tipped leaves turn red at maturity.

Political cartoonists frequently use this name as a subject of their drawings but more often than not they represent it as a true thistle of the Family Compositae rather than of its correct family, - Chenepodiaceae. Let's hope the cartoonists' knowledge of world affairs is more accurate than their botany.

9b Leaves lanceolate; carpels 5, styles 5; fruit a many-seeded capsule (dry dehiscent fruit of several carpels). Fig. 68.

DITCH STONECROP *Penthorum sedoides* L.

Figure 68

It grows to a height of ½ to 2 feet and is found in low places, ditches and swamps. Leaves alternate, serrate, 2 to 4 inches long. The tiny, inconspicuous flowers are greenish-white to yellowish and 10 to 12 somewhat elongated stamens; the petals are sometimes absent.

10a Stipules dry and silvery, tapering to a point (a); **leaves opposite;** fruit a one-seeded utricle. Fig. 69.

FORKING WHITLOW-WORT *Paronychia virginica* **Spreng.**

Figure 69

A rather inconspicuous member of the Knotwort Family (also called Whitlow-wort Family) found flowering from July to October in dry soil. This smooth, much-branched plant (4-14 inches high) arises from a rather woody base and bears narrow opposite bristle-tipped leaves and stipules which may be ½ inch long.

Tiny white or greenish flowers are clustered in open, repeatedly-forking cymes. Sepals are 5, stamens 5, and style 2-cleft. In place of petals, there are 5 minute bristles.

10b **Stipules in the form of sheaths (Fig. 70a.); leaves alternate; fruit an achene (small, dry one-celled, one-seeded indehiscent fruit).** 11

Figure 70

11a **Prickle-armed, reclining-climbing plants with angled stems; leaves** hastate or arrow-shaped. 12

11b **Plants not armed with prickles; stems not angled; leaves heart-shaped, ovate, lanceolate, or linear.** 13

12a **Leaves mostly broadly hastate, with long petioles; stem grooved-angled. Fig. 71.**

HALBERD-LEAVED TEAR-THUMB *Polygonum arifolium* **L.**

Figure 71

A fairly common reclining plant (2-6 feet long) of low ground with the leaves one to 10 inches long and small inconspicuous rose or greenish flowers in terminal or axillary clusters. Usually there are 6 stamens and 2 styles. The dark-brown shining achene is lenticular (biconvex).

As in the following species the stem is armed with prickles which inflict vicious wounds if the plant is grasped in the hand. Another common name is Scratch-grass. Both names are appropriate as anyone with first-hand experience will agree.

12b Leaves sagittate, with short petioles; stem 4-angled. Fig. 72.
    ARROW-LEAVED TEAR-THUMB *Polygonum sagittatum* L.

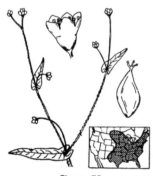

Figure 72

This weak slender species climbs over other plants by means of the sharp downward-pointing prickles which arm the stem. The arrow-shaped leaves (1-3 inches long) are short-petioled or sometimes sessile.

The small pink to greenish flowers are in dense terminal clusters. Usually each blossom has a 5-parted calyx, 8 stamens, and 3 styles. The 3-angled achene is smooth and shining. You'll find this fairly common plant growing in wet soil and flowering from July to October.

13a Plant twining; leaves heart-shaped. Fig. 73.
    CLIMBING FALSE BUCKWHEAT *Polygonum scandens* L.

Figure 73

A widely distributed rather decorative vine (4-20 feet long) found in woods and along roadsides climbing over rocks and other plants. The ovate to cordate leaves (1-6 inches long) have sharp-pointed tips and heart-shaped bases. The greenish or whitish flowers are borne in numerous panicled racemes. The 3-angled achene is smooth and shining. Flowering from July to September.

Some other members of the Buckwheat Family are Dock, Sheep Sorrel, Prince's Feather, Lady's Thumb, Black Bindweed, Buckwheat, Rhubarb.

13b Plant erect or somewhat decumbent; leaves linear, lanceolate, or ovate. **14**

14a Leaves linear, decidous (falling off); flowers on solitary pedicels in panicled racemes. Fig. 74.

COAST JOINTWEED *Polygonella articulata* (L.)

Figure 74

Look for this interesting member of the Buckwheat family in sandy places along the coast or near the Great Lakes. The jointed slender wiry stem bears very narrow alternate sessile leaves, which soon fall off, and small flowers in numerous slender racemes. The white or pinkish blossoms appear exceedingly dainty on their solitary nodding pedicels. Usually the calyx is 5-parted, the stamens number 8, and the styles are 3. In bloom from July to October.

14b Leaves lanceolate to ovate, persistent; flowers in loose or dense spikes. **15**

15a Calyx usually 4-parted; stipules with a marginal fringe of bristles (a); flowers in loose, slender spikes (4-12 inches long). Fig. 75.

VIRGINIA KNOTWEED *Tovara virginiana* (L.)

Figure 75

A fairly common glabrous or pubescent member of the Buckwheat Family growing in rich woods. Plant (1-4 feet tall) erect or arching bearing ovate to elliptical sharp-pointed leaves and tiny greenish-pink flowers (about 1/10 inch broad) scattered in very slender axillary or terminal stalks. Usually the flower consists of a 4-parted calyx, 4 stamens, and a pistil with 2 exserted styles.

The stipules in Family Polygonaceae are sheath-like above the swollen joints of the stem. In this particular species the edges of the cylindrical stipules are fringed with bristles.

15b Calyx usually 5-parted; stipules not fringed on the margin; flowers in one or two dense racemes (1-3 inches long). Fig. 76.

SWAMP SMARTWEED *Polygonum coccineum* Muhl.

A decumbent or nearly erect weedy plant (1-3 feet tall) usually growing in low ground, often in mud. The thinnish, ovate-lanceolate to lanceolate leaves (2-8 inches long) are narrowly acuminate; the stipules are cylindrical and are not fringed on the margin.

Generally one or two dense racemes of dark rose-colored flowers are present. Each flower has a 5-parted calyx, 5 exserted stamens, and an exserted 2-cleft style. The achene is black and shining. Blooms from July to October.

Figure 76

16a Plants with milky bitter juice; flowers in a calyx-like involucre with many staminate flowers (each of a single stamen) and one pistillate flower (a 3-lobed pistil), the entire structure likely to be mistaken for a flower. Fig. 77. 17

Figure 77

16b Plants without milky juice; flowers with a true calyx. 22

17a All the leaves opposite; involucres solitary in the axils or in axillary cymes. 18

17b Upper leaves whorled or opposite, lower leaves scattered or alternate; involucres in a usually terminal umbel-like inflorescense, often showy. 20

18a Plant erect; appendages of the involucral glands broad and conspicuous. Fig. 78.

LARGE SPOTTED SPURGE *Euphorbia maculata* L.

Figure 78

This is often an abundant weed in gardens, fields and waste places and attains a height of ½ to 2 feet. It is often much branched and spreading. The rather-narrow, roughly-serrate leaves are mottled and blotched with red. The small flowers are white but often bear some red markings.

The Spurge Family (Euphorbiaceae) to which this and the seven following plants belong, is a large and important family. Many species have milky sap and the family may frequently be readily recognized by the large ovary (pistillate flower) which is borne on an elongated stem and hangs out at one side of the cup bearing the staminate flowers, as pictured. (See Fig. 80a).

18b Plant prostrate-spreading; appendages of the involucral glands minute or none. 19

19a Plant glabrous; leaves entire; seed smooth. Fig. 79.

SEASIDE SPURGE *Euphorbia polygonifolia* L.

This prostrate, smooth, pale-green annual is a shore weed growing along the Great Lakes and the Atlantic coast. The less-than-an-inch-long entire leaves are borne in pairs on stems that seldom exceed 8 inches in length. The flowers are inconspicuous except for the ovary. Another name is Shore Spurge.

Figure 79

19b Plant hairy; leaves toothed; seeds rough. Fig. 80.

MILK PURSLANE *Euphorbia supina* Raf.

This close-growing dark-green annual is covered with a heavy coat of rather long hairs. The stems and small serrate leaves are usually blotched with red. The tiny flowers are white or red with the hair-covered ovary the most conspicuous part.

Just why the "milk" should be emphasized for this species is not apparent as many of the members of this large genus (over 1000 world-wide) possess thick milky sap.

Figure 80

20a Uppermost leaves petal-like with conspicuous white margins; capsule pubescent. Fig. 81.

SNOW-ON-THE-MOUNTAIN *Euphorbia marginata* Pursh.

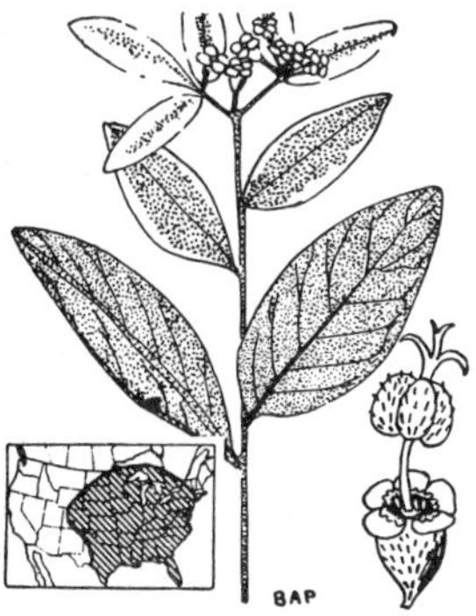

This sturdy-growing plant is a common pasture and open ground weed in our West and Northwest but in many other areas is a prized dooryard ornamental. The inflorescence of white margined flowers is surrounded by a whorl of leaves, green with broad white margins, which makes the plant conspicuous. It grows to a height of 2 feet.

MEXICAN FIRE-PLANT *E. heterophylla*, which some contend should be called "Fire-On-The-Mountain", has an involucre of green and bright red bracts. It grows to a height of 2 to 3 feet, from Illinois to S. Dakota and Texas.

Figure 81

20b Leaves not petal-like; capsule smooth (not hairy). 21
21a Leaves entire; seeds slightly pitted. Fig. 82.

FLOWERING SPURGE *Euphorbia corollata* L.

This really attractive roadside weed has conspicuous flowers in widely spreading double umbels which arise from a whorl of leaf-like bracts. It grows to a height of 2 to 3 feet.

POINSETTIA *E. pulcherrima*, the well-known Christmas plant should have been mentioned under 20a. This native of the tropics is grown out of doors in our warmer areas and is a well-known greenhouse and pot plant.

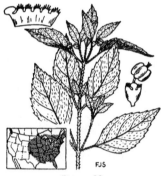

Figure 82

21b Leaves coarsely toothed; seeds tubercled (with projections or bumps). Fig. 83.

TOOTHED SPURGE *Euphorbia dentata* Michx.

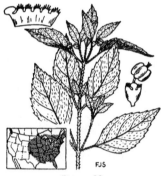

It is a dull green pubescent annual with more conspicuous leaves than many other members of the genus, some of them measuring up to 3 or 4 inches in length and being sometimes half as wide as long. The leaves have prominent serrations. The yellowish flowers are small and inconspicuous.

Figure 83

22a Ovary 2 to 3 celled; fruit a capsule with 2 or more seeds. Fig. 84. 23

Figure 84

22b Ovary one-celled; fruit an achene or utricle, one-seeded. Fig. 85. 24

Figure 85

23a Leaves long-petioled; large leaf-like cut-lobed bracts subtending the pistillate and staminate flowers (a); stigmas 3, much-branched. Fig. 86.

VIRGINIA THREE-SEEDED MERCURY *Acalypha virginica* L.

Figure 86

This ½ to 2 foot tall, rather delicate plant is often purplish tinged. The heavily serrated leaves measure up to 3 inches or more in length. The small yellowish-green staminate and pistillate flowers are together borne in a prominent fringed bract in the axils of the leaves, as pictured.

HORNBEAM THREE-SEEDED MERCURY *A. ostryaefolia* Ridd., somewhat taller and ranging from N. J. to Mex., has cordate leaves and the staminate and pistillate flowers borne in separate spikes.

23b Leaves sessile or nearly so; floral bracts small, simple (a); stigmas 3, not branched. Fig. 87.

QUEEN'S DELIGHT *Stillingia sylvatica* L.

Figure 87

This 1 to 3 foot fleshy perennial has leaves measuring up to 4 inches. The small flowers are borne in terminal spikes, the staminate ones being placed above the pistillate flowers. The root has medicinal uses.

CASTOR-BEAN *Ricinus communis* L., a tropical perennial, raised as an ornamental annual in temperate regions has conspicuous 5 to 11 palmately-lobed leaves. Castor oil is made from its "beans".

24a Leaves entire; flowers small, in dry and scarious (thin and dry, not green), axillary or terminal spiked clusters. 25

24b Leaves toothed; flowers small, mostly axillary, not dry and scarious. 26

25a Plant rough and usually pubescent; leaves ovate, acute or acuminate; stamens and sepals usually 5. Fig. 88a.
GREEN AMARANTH *Amaranthus retroflexus* L.

Figure 88

A coarse rough definitely weedy plant (1-9 feet tall) now common in cultivated and waste places throughout North America where it has been introduced from tropical America. Flowers greenish in thick stiff bristly spikes. Also called Rough Pigweed. The numerous common names of this and the following species are more or less interchangeable.

SLENDER PIGWEED *Amaranthus hybridus* L., Fig. 88b is a similar species but darker green and with more-slender flowering spikes. The familiar Cockscomb of flower gardens is a close relative.

25b Plant smooth and glabrous; leaves obovate to spatulate, obtuse; stamens and sepals usually 3. Fig. 89.
TUMBLE-WEED *Amaranthus graecizans* L.

Figure 89

A widespread weedy plant (6-20 inches high) of roadsides, fields, and waste places with slender whitish branches, slender-petioled leaves (½ to 1½ inches long) and small greenish flowers.

The leaves drop away in the autumn, leaving a stiff wiry skeleton which is tumbled and blown by the wind, spreading seeds as it goes. Often great numbers of these leafless Tumble-weeds can be seen piled up along a fence where their uncertain journey has temporarily deposited them.

26a Plants with stinging hairs. 27

26b Plants without stinging hairs. 28

27a Leaves alternate, ovate; flowers usually 5-parted. Fig. 90.

WOOD NETTLE *Laportea canadensis* (L.)

A stout plant (2-4 feet high) armed with stinging hairs and bearing thin long-petioled, sharp-toothed leaves and greenish flowers in loose branched clusters. It is rare near the coast but generally common in the rest of its range. Flowering from July to September in rich woods.

Some other members of the Nettle Family are Elm, Mulberry, Hackberry, Osage Orange, Hop.

Figure 90

27b Leaves opposite, lanceolate to lanceolate-ovate; flowers 4-parted.

Fig. 91.   ### SLENDER WILD NETTLE *Urtica gracilis* Ait.

A common, apparently native plant (2-7 feet tall) of waste places and moist ground with narrow, sharply-toothed leaves and numerous greenish inconspicuous flowers in loose axillary panicles. This usually slender plant has considerably fewer stinging hairs than the following species but even so is unpleasant to encounter.

STINGING NETTLE *Urtica dioica* L. (2-4 feet tall) is a stouter broader-leaved plant than the above species and is densely armed with stinging hairs which produce an itching burning sensation if brushed against the skin. A native of Europe and Asia, now naturalized in many of our states.

Figure 91

28a Stigma with many hair-like branches (a); flower clusters shorter than leaf-stalks; plants weak, clear and transparent, succulent (juicy). Fig. 92. CLEARWEED *Pilea pumila* (L.)

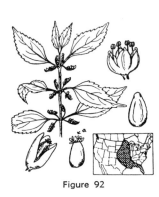

Figure 92

This rather weak, juicy plant (6-20 inches high) has an appropriate common name because it is clear and transparent. Growing in cool moist shady places, often on old logs, it quickly wilts when picked. The ovate, coarsely-toothed leaves are prominently 3-veined and have slender petioles. The numerous greenish inconspicuous flowers grow in small clusters at the base of the leaf stalks and are shorter than them. Another popular name for this common plant usually found blooming from July to September, is Coolweed. It also grows in Japan.

28b Stigma long and hair-like (a); flower clusters usually longer than leaf-stalks; stem stiff; plant not noticeably succulent. Fig. 93. FALSE NETTLE *Boehmeria cylindrica* (L.)

Figure 93

A rough-pubescent or nearly smooth, erect plant (1-3 feet high) of moist shady places belong to the Nettle Family but without stinging hairs. The coarsely-toothed thin ovate to ovate-lanceolate leaves (1-3½ inches long) are usually opposite on the stiff stem.

The small greenish flowers are borne in axillary spikes, some of which have staminate flowers only, some pistillate flowers only, while other spikes contain both kinds of flowers. Generally the staminate spikes are interrupted, the pistillate mostly continuous, often with small leaves at the tip. Flowering from July to September. Also found in the West Indies.

44

29a Petals separate from each other (in *Oxalis* and *Limonium* the petals are sometimes slightly united). Fig. 94. 30

Figure 94

29b Petals at least partly united (Fig. 95); (only slightly united in *Asclepias, Ampelamus, Sicyos, Echinocystis)*; (the two lower petals of most Leguminosae are usually united (a); (the lateral pair on each side united in *Impatiens*). 71

Figure 95

30a Stamens numerous, at least more than 10 and more than twice the number of sepals or calyx lobes. Fig. 96. 31

Figure 96

30b Stamens not more than twice the number of petals (Fig. 97); *(Agrimonia* with 5 petals has from 5 to 15 stamens, *Lechea* with 3 petals has from 3 to 12 stamens.)......39

Figure 97

31a Pistils several or many, wholly distinct or united at base in a strongly-lobed or several-beaked ovary. Fig. 98. 32

Figure 98

31b Pistils strictly one as to ovary; styles or stigmas 2 to 5. Fig. 99. 34

Figure 99

32a Pistils 11 or more, in a ring; flowers yellow, mostly axillary; leaves velvety-pubescent. Fig. 100.

Figure 100

VELVET LEAF *Abutilon theophrasti* Medic.
One of the best-known annual weeds which grows to a height of 2 to 4 feet. The large heart-shaped leaves (4-12 inches) and stems are covered with a soft velvety pubescence. The yellow flowers are ½ to almost 1 inch across; the fruit, as pictured, has given the plant the name "Butter Print". The stems are sturdy and contain very tough fibers giving it another name, "Indian Hemp".
The seeds of this plant are highly resistant and have been germinated after being kept for 60 years. It grows only in rich soil, but once established it comes up year after year even though none of the plants are permitted to mature seeds.

32b Pistils 3 to 8, not in a ring; flowers white or blue, racemed or panicled; leaves not velvety-pubescent. 33

33a Flowers regular, white, in a long feathery raceme; leaves de-compound. Fig. 101.
          AMERICAN BUGBANE *Cimicifuga americana* Michx.

Figure 101

This slender-stemmed perennial herb arises from a thick rootstalk to a height of 3 to 5 feet. The leaves are twice compound; the flowers are borne in pubescent compound racemes 1 to 2 feet long. They are white and measure nearly ½ inch across. The fruit is a follicle becoming about ½ inch long.

Two other species of this genus bloom in spring or summer. They belong to the Crowfoot family.

33b Flowers irregular, blue, in a loose panicle; leaves simple, 3 to 5 lobed. Fig. 102.   **WILD MONKSHOOD *Aconitum uncinatum* L.**

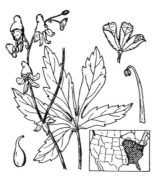

Figure 102

This weak usually-climbing perennial herb has a length of 2 to 4 feet. The deeply-lobed leaves are broader than long. The blue flowers are about 1 inch across and are borne in a panicle; each flower produces 3 follicles, a little over ½ inch long. It is found in the woods.

The name "Monkshood" refers to the pouched overhanging upper sepal; the term "Wolfsbane", sometimes applied to this genus comes from the use of the root in poisoning wolves.

34a Leaves alternate; stamens forming a column around the pistil (Fig. 103); flowers usually pink, 4 to 7 inches broad...35

Figure 103

34b Leaves opposite; stamens not in a column but often in clusters of 3 or 5; flowers yellow less than 1½ inches broad. 36

35a Leaves densely pubescent beneath; petals rose-color; seeds glabrous. Fig. 104.   SWAMP ROSE MALLOW *Hibiscus moscheutos* **L.**

This sturdy-growing very showy plant is found at the edge of waterways or in brackish marshes where it arises from a perennial root to a height of 3 to 7 feet. The leaves are velvety-tomentose and vary from lanceolate to broad and often lobed forms. The rather numerous and attractive pink flowers measure up to 7 inches or more in width.

Figure 104

35b Leaves glabrous on both sides; petals flesh-color with dark bases; seeds hairy. Fig. 105.

HALBERD-LEAVED ROSE MALLOW *Hibiscus militaris* **Cav.**

This is a smaller plant than the preceding seldom attaining a height of more than 5 feet. The lower and often other leaves are halbert-shaped in keeping with the name. The flowers do not open so wide, are somewhat smaller and have a dark eye. The capsule is enclosed in the calyx; the seeds are silk-covered instead of being glabrous as in *moscheutos*.

Hibiscus is a large genus of almost 300 species many of which are tropical and often very showy.

Figure 105

36a Sepals 4, in two unequal pairs; petals 4; styles 2. Fig. 106.

ST. ANDREW'S CROSS *Ascyrum hypericoides* **L.**

This interesting dry-soil plant attains a height of less than a foot. The stems are flattened and the opposite leaves are narrow and measure ½ to 1½ inches long. The flowers are pale yellow, somewhat less than an inch across and are both terminal and axillary.

It and the three species which follow belong to the St. John's-wort family which may usually be easily recognized by the very numerous fine stamens. It has some 300 members.

Figure 106

36b Sepals 5; petals 5; styles 3. ....**37**

37a Petals black-dotted on the margin; leaves less than one inch long; flowers 2/3 to one inch broad; capsule 3-celled. Fig. 107.
COMMON ST. JOHN'S-WORT *Hypericum perforatum* L.

This herbaceous perennial arises from a woody base to a possible height of 3 feet. The leaves are opposite, sessile and thickly dotted with black. The sepals and the bright yellow petals also have many black dots. The capsules are ovoid, 3-celled and about ¼ inch long. It has been introduced from Europe and is found in dry fields and in waste places.

Figure 107

37b Petals without black dots; leaves over one inch long; flowers 1/3 to 2/3 inch broad; capsule one-celled. **38**

38a Styles united below; stigmas elongate; flowers bright yellow. Fig. 108.
ROUND-PODDED ST. JOHN'S-WORT *Hypericum sphaerocarpum* Michx.

The 4-angled stems of this plant grow to a height of about 2 feet; the leaves are from 1½ to 3 inches long but comparitively narrow. The numerous yellow flowers are borne in large terminal cymes. The styles are 3, the slender stamens very numerous and the capsule but 1-celled.

Figure 108

38b Styles distinct; stigmas capitate; flowers copper-yellow. Fig. 109.
COPPER-COLORED ST. JOHN'S-WORT Hypericum denticulatum
acutifolium (Ell.)

Figure 109

This low-grounds slender plant may attain a height of about 2 feet. The stems are 4-angled; the leaves usually small and the numerous copper-colored flowers around ½ inch broad. There are 3 distinct styles and the small capsule has but one cell. it is enclosed within the persistent calyx.

39a Ovary inferior (epigynous — below the calyx).
Fig. 110. 40

Figure 110

39b Ovary superior (hypogynous—above the calyx). (Par
nassia is sometimes partly inferior; Rhexia appears inferior but is superior.) Fig. 111. 50

Figure 111

40a Flowers in dense scaly heads; leaves mostly near the base, parallel-veined, elongate-linear with bristly margins. Fig. 112.
RATTLESNAKE MASTER Eryngium yuccifolium Michx.

Figure 112

This very interesting plant, frequently listed as an aquatic and given the specific name of *aquaticum* by Linnaeus is very often found in upland prairie situations. It grows to a height of 2 to 5 feet; the species name is well taken, for its leaves are that of the Yucca all over again. The flowering heads as well as the whole plant are harsh. The flowers are greenish-white.

40b Flowers in umbels, racemes, spikes, or axillary, but not in dense heads; leaves mostly alternate (opposite in *Circaea*), simple or compound. **41**

41a Flowers in umbels; leaves compound (in *Oxypolis* sometimes reduced to hollow cylindrical petioles); styles 2. Fig. 113. ....**42**

Figure 113

41b Flowers racemed, axillary, or in spikes; leaves simple; style united into one. Fig. 114. ....**45**

Figure 114

42a Fruit flattened laterally (from side to side); involucre (a) dissected or with numerous bracts. Fig. 115. ....**43**

Figure 115

42b Fruit flattened dorsally (from back to front), the lateral ribs prominently winged (Fig. 116a); involucre none, deciduous (falling off), or of a few small bracts. **44**

Figure 116

43a Plant stout, 2 to 6 feet high; leaves once-pinnate (lower leaves often much-dissected). Fig. 117.

HEMLOCK WATER PARSNIP *Sium suave* Walt.

Figure 117

This is one of the aquatic members of the Parsley family, which grows in ponds, marshes and swamps, to a height of 2 to 5 feet. The leaves are finely cut as pictured; the white flowers are borne in compound umbels. The fruit is compressed and has sturdy ribs.

FLORIDA WATER PARSNIP *S. floridanum* Small, growing in similar habitats in Florida is smaller and more slender.

43b Plant slender, one to 3 feet high; leaves finely dissected into thread-like segments. Fig. 118.

MOCK BISHOP-WEED *Ptilimnium capillaceum* **(Michx.)**

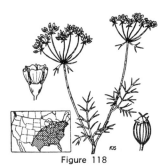

This weak, scantily-leafed plant grows to a height of 1 to 2 feet and is found in wet soil especially in brackish areas. The white flowers grow in compound umbels. The small flattened fruit is about as wide as long.

P. costatum (Ell.) a taller plant but with narrow sepals is found in coastal plain swamps of the Southeast.

Figure 118

44a Leaves one-pinnate; calyx teeth evident; lateral wings of fruit touching (b). Fig. 119.

COWBANE *Oxypolis rigidior* **(L.)**

It is a slender-growing, white-flowered plant found in swamps and attaining a height of 2 to 6 feet. The compound leaves are pale on their under side. The flowers and fruit are borne in compound umbels. The thickened rootstalk from which it grows has given it the name "Pig-Potato".

Figure 119

44b Leaves several times pinnate; calyx teeth obsolete (not **evident or** ridimentary); lateral wings of fruit spreading (a). Fig. 120.

HEMLOCK PARSLEY *Conioselinum chinense* **(L.)**

This plant is found in cold swamps and on wet cliffs. The leaves are much compounded as pictured. The fruit is prominently ribbed, much flattened and definitely longer than wide. The petals are white.

The Parsley Family (Umbelliferae) is a large and important one. Many valuable food plants are included in it as well as a few very poisonous ones.

Figure 120

45a Petals 2; stamens 2; leaves opposite, ovate. Fig. 121.
  SMALLER ENCHANTER'S NIGHTSHADE *Circaea alpina* L.

It is often common in moist woods where it grows to a height of a foot or less. The coarsely dentate opposite leaves are 1 to 2 inches in length. The flowers have but 2 sepals, 2 petals and 2 stamens and are borne in racemes. The petals are white; the ovoid fruit is covered with soft hairs and but one celled.

ENCHANTER'S NIGHTSHADE C. *quadrisulcata* (Maxim.) growing about twice as tall as the preceding, with considerably larger fruit, has much the same range and habitat. Its fruit is two celled.

Figure 121

45b Petals usually 4; stamens 4, 6 or 8; leaves mostly alternate, lanceolate. 46

46a Flowers yellow, ½ to 2½ inches broad. 47

46b Flowers white, pink, or purple, 1/6 to 1 1/3 inches broad. 48

47a Stamens 8; flowers in terminal bracted spikes; capsules pubescent.
  Fig. 122. **COMMON EVENING PRIMROSE** *Oenothera biennis* L.

A sturdy hirsute biennial growing to a possible height of 5 feet along roadsides, in neglected fields, etc. The slightly dentate, lanceolate leaves range up to 6 inches in length; the lower ones possess stems but most of the leaves are sessile. The bright yellow flowers open in the evening and are 1 to 2½ inches broad. It is sometimes raised as an ornamental as are several other species of the Evening-primrose Family.

Figure 122

47b Stamens usually 4; flowers axillary; capsules glabrous. Fig. 123.
  SEEDBOX *Ludwigia alternifolia* L.

This 2 to 4 foot plant with alternate lanceolate leaves and yellow petals grows in swamps and other wet places. The solitary flowers, ½ inch or more across, are borne in the axils of the leaves. The fruit is a somewhat cube-shaped capsule less than ½ inch long, which gives the plant its common name. The roots are often enlarged into tubers. The genus has more than 20 American species.

Figure 123

48a Fruit nutlike, 1 to 4 seeded, indehiscent (not opening to discharge seeds) or nearly so. Fig. 124.

BIENNIAL GAURA *Gaura biennis* L.

In many regions this is a common roadside weed which grows to a height of 2 to 5 feet and is much branched. The partly pubescent, lanceolate leaves are 2 to 4 inches long. The flowers are borne in long slender spikes and are almost ½ inch across; they are at first white but presently turn to pink. The fruit, a small sessile capsule, is narrowed at each end; it has 4 longitudinal ridges and is covered with a sticky pubescence.

Figure 124

48b Fruit a capsule that opens to discharge its numerous seeds.... 49

49a Calyx tube prolonged beyond the ovary; flowers 1/3 inch or less broad, pink or white; stigma usually entire. Fig. 125.

PURPLE-LEAVED WILLOW-HERB *Epilobium coloratum* Muhl.

The stems and leaves of this much-branched bushy plant are often tinged with purple; the plant has a height of 1 to 3 feet and the leaves are 2 to 5 inches long. The many flowers are borne in the leaf axils and are white or pink and are generally nodding; the petals are usually notched. The calyx tube, in contrast to the next species extends beyond the ovary. It grows in low, wet places.

Figure 125

49b Calyx tube not prolonged beyond the ovary; flowers 2/3 to 1 1/3 inches broad, reddish-purple (rarely white); stigma 4-lobed. Fig. 126.

FIREWEED *Epilobium angustifolium* L.

This plant grows from 2 to 8 feet high and has alternate, lanceolate leaves up to 6 inches long. The flowers are 1 inch or more across; the petals are purple or sometimes white and are not notched as in the preceding species, nor does the calyx tube extend beyond the ovary. It grows in open woods and comes in quickly and in great abundance in burned over areas; this accounts for its common name.

Figure 126

53

50a **Plants with scale-like leaves.** 51
50b **Plants with true leaves.** 52
51a **Plant a yellowish or reddish saprophyte; flowers few in a raceme; style one. Fig. 127.**   PINESAP *Monotropa hypopithys* L.

The members of this genus live as saprophytes in places where there is quantities of decaying organic matter. This species is lemon yellow or pinkish, is covered with a fine pubescence and grows to a height of 4 inches to 1 foot. The leaves are reduced to scales; the flowers are bell-shaped and almost an inch long. The oval capsule is 1/3 inch long or more. It grows in rich woods. It is also known as False Beech-drops and as Yellowbird's-nest.

Figure 127

51b **Plant not saprophytic although orange-colored in the fall; flowers scattered along the branches; styles 3. Fig. 128.**

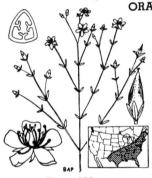

ORANGE-GRASS *Hypericum gentianoides* (L.)
This scaly-stemmed plant grows in sandy soil to a height of 4 to 18 inches. The tiny yellow or orange flowers have 3 styles and 5-10 stamens. The 3-parted capsule is conical and less than ¼ inch long. The flowers have a breadth of about ¼ inch.

DRUMMOND'S ORANGE-GRASS *H. drummondii* G. & H. is similar but its deep-yellow flowers are twice as large, have 10 to 20 stamens and are borne on pedicels instead of being sessile.

Figure 128

52a **Sepals 5, two of them smaller and more narrow than the other 3; petals 3. Fig. 129.**

THYME-LEAVED PIN-WEED *Lechea minor* L.

This plant grows in dry open ground and has a height of 6 to 20 inches. The stem-leaves are up to ½ inch long and oval; the upper leaves are smaller and narrower. The small flowers have 2 outer narrow sepals and 3 inner broader ones. The 3 petals are purplish-red. The small, oval, three-parted capsule usually contains 6 seeds.

Figure 129

52b Calyx lobes or sepals usually 4 or 5 and all alike; petals 4 or 5 or occasionally up to 8 (*Drosera* rarely has one to 3 petals). 53

53a Leaves whorled or opposite. Fig. 130. 54

Figure 130

53b Leaves alternate or basal. Fig. 131. 58

Figure 131

54a Leaves entire (not toothed or divided). Fig. 132. 55

Figure 132

54b Leaves toothed or deeply 3 to 5 divided. Fig. 133....57

Figure 133

55a Styles 2; stamens free, not attached to calyx; stem swollen at the nodes (a). Fig. 134.

Figure 134

BOUNCING BET *Saponaria officinalis* L.

This vigorous-growing roadside plant is of European origin and was introduced here as an ornamental from which it often escapes. Double flowered forms are rather common. The sap makes a suds in water, hence the name "Soapwort". It grows to a height of 1 to 2 feet, with oval leaves 1 to 3 inches long. The flowers are about 1 inch across and pinkish or white.

55b Style one; stamens attached to calyx; stem not enlarged at nodes. 56

56a Flowers regular or nearly so; plant smooth or somewhat pubescent, growing in swampy places. Fig. 135.

SWAMP LOOSESTRIFE *Decodon verticillatus* (L.)

Figure 135

This aquatic perennial with angular stems grows in ponds and swamps to a height of 3 to 10 feet. The short petioled lanceolate leaves are from 2 to 5 inches long. The pinkish-purple flowers, about 1 inch across, are borne in axilary cymes. The fruit is a capsule about ¼ inch across. Another name is Willow-herb.

56b Flowers irregular; plant clammy-pubescent, growing in dry soil. Fig. 136.

CLAMMY CUPHEA *Cuphea petiolata* (L.)

Figure 136

This purple flowered annual is found in dry soil and stands at a height of 6 to 20 inches. The lanceolate leaves with long slim petioles are opposite or sometimes whorled. The flowers have short peduncles and are borne in the leaf axils; they are about 1/3 inch across. The capsule is unusual in that it ruptures before the seeds are ripe and the placenta projects outward until the seeds are mature.

57a Petals 4; stamens 8; leaves ovate, finely toothed; calyx tube urn-shaped. Fig. 137.

MEADOW-BEAUTY *Rhexia virginica* L.

Figure 137

This plant is found in damp meadows and sandy swamps; it grows with few or no branches to a height of a foot or more. The leaves are opposite and 1 to 2 inches long. The flowers, 1 to 1½ inches across, have four bright purple petals; they are borne in cymes. The whole plant is sometimes red.

MARYLAND MEADOW-BEAUTY *R. mariana* L., with paler flowers and round instead of square stems, ranges from Long Island to Texas.

56

57b Petals 5; stamens 10; leaves deeply 3 to 5 divided, the divisions cut and toothed; calyx of 5 separate sepals. Fig. 138.

HERB ROBERT *Geranium robertianum* L.

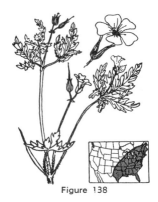

This is a much-branched weak glandular-villous plant which is found in rocky woods and attains a height of a foot or more. The leaves are finely cut as pictured and heavily scented. The reddish-purple flowers, about ½ inch broad are borne in pairs. Another name is Red-robin.

Figure 138

58a Sepals 4; petals 4; stamens 6. Fig. 139. 59

Figure 139

58b Not as in 58a. 61

59a Fleshy seaside plant; flowers purplish; seed-pod transversely 2-jointed (a). Fig. 140.

AMERICAN SEA ROCKET *Cakile edentula* (Bigel.)

This fleshy member of the Mustard Family grows in sand along the seashore and the shores of lakes and is about a foot high. The flowers are light purple and about ¼ inch across. The fruit is a short, two-jointed pod, with one seed in each part or sometimes only in the upper joint.

Figure 140

59b Plant not fleshy; flowers white or yellow; seed-pod continuous, not transversely jointed. 60

60a Flowers white; pods triangular, spreading. Fig. 141.

SHEPHERD'S PURSE *Capsella bursa-pastoris* (L.)

Figure 141

The triangular pods, about ¼ inch across, are perhaps the most characteristic thing about this plant. It begins blooming when only a few inches high and may stretch up to nearly 2 feet, much of this length being in the long drawn-out raceme. The flowers are white; a pod bears around 20 seeds in its two cells. This plant has been found in bloom out of doors in Iowa every month in the year.

WILD PEPPERGRASS *Lepidium virginicum* L. (141b) is another very common mustard often flowering from Spring through Fall. It can be distinguished from the above by its circular fruit.

60b Flowers yellow; pods linear, closely appressed to the stem.
Fig. 142. **HEDGE MUSTARD** *Sisymbrium officinale* (L.)

Figure 142

Like the above, this plant is an introduced European weed. It is readily recognized by its slim compact growth; it may reach a height of 3 feet. The plant is somewhat pubescent; the tiny four-petalled flowers are bright yellow and the pods, becoming about ½ inch long are closely appressed to the stem.

61a Leaves mostly basal or appearing so.
Fig. 143. ....**62**

Figure 143

61b Leaves alternate. Fig. 144. ....**66**

Figure 144

62a Insectivorous plant; leaves elongate, thread-like, covered with sticky hairs. Fig. 145.

THREAD-LEAVED SUNDEW *Drosera filiformis* Raf.

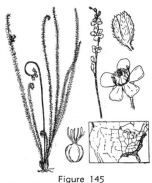

This odd-appearing plant grows in wet sand in coastal areas. The smooth flowering stem may reach a height of 20 inches and bears 10 to 25 flowers in a 1-sided raceme. The flowers are purple and have a breadth of ¼ to 1 inch. The leaves all arise from the base and are twisted filiform structures 5 to 15 inches long and are covered with a glandular pubescence.

This genus of insectivorous plants is at its best in Australia where many species are known.

Figure 145

62b Plants not insectivorous; leaves broad, not thread-like. 63

63a Leaves palmately divided into narrow segments; flower irregular, purple or lavender. Fig. 146. BIRD-FOOT VIOLET *Viola pedata* L.

This is one of the most striking of all our violets. It first blooms in the spring but has another round at it in the fall. The flowers are often an inch or more across and usually have the two upper petals deep velvety purple and the other three pale lavender but in one variety all the petals are lavender. The leaves are finely cut.

Figure 146

63b Leaves entire; flower regular, greenish-white or pale purple.....64

64a Flowers many, small (about ⅛ inch broad), lavender. Fig. 147.

SEA LAVENDER *Limonium carolinianum* (Walt.)

Growing to a height of 6 to 20 inches from a thickened root, this glabrous herb is found in sand dunes, meadows and salt-marshes. The leaves are oblanceolate, entire or with wavy edge and 3 to 10 inches long. The flowers are small and numerous; the pale purple petals are spatulate.

The genus is a large one with a number of introduced species being raised as ornamentals. They are often used in dry bouquets.

Figure 147

59

64b Flowers few (¾ to 1½ inches broad), greenish-white. 65

65a Petals sessile; leaf-blades ovate to orbicular (circular). Fig. 148.
CAROLINA GRASS-OF-PARNASSUS *Parnassia glauca* Raf.

This interesting and rather rare plant grows in bogs and swamps and becomes abundant when conditions are just right. The basal leaves resemble those of the plantains; the flowering scape becomes 6 to 20 inches high and has a sessile clasping leaf below the middle. The flowers, an inch or more in width, have white petals with greenish veins.

Figure 148

65b Petals clawed (a); leaf-blades reniform to orbicular-reniform.
Fig. 149.
KIDNEY-LEAVED GRASS-OF-PARNASSUS *Parnassia asarifolia* Vent.

This species differs from the foregoing in having leafblades wider than long, and petals with claws. It belongs quite largely to the mountains and grows in wet places. The flowers are about an inch broad and are greenish-white.

NORTHERN GRASS-OF-PARNASSUS *P. palustris* L. is smaller than either of the above species. It grows on our northern border, in Canada and west in the Rockies.

Figure 149

66a Flowers pinkish; pistils 4 or 5; leaves simple, fleshy. Fig. 150.
AMERICAN ORPINE *Sedum telephioides* Michx.

This native "Wild Live-forever" is highly similar to the species (*S. triphyllum* (Haw.)) introduced from Europe and often seen in dooryards. This is a smaller, more delicate plant than its European cousin. The coarsely dentate leaves are 1 to 2 inches long; the flowers have all their parts in fives; the petals are pinkish.

Figure 150

66b Flowers yellow, pistils one or 2; leaves compound, not fleshy....67

67a Leaves palmately-compound with 3 leaflets; calyx of 5 separate sepals; plants with sour sap. Fig. 151.

UPRIGHT YELLOW WOOD SORREL *Oxalis stricta* L.

Figure 151

This low pale-green plant grows erect to a height of about 6 inches. The leaves with their 3 heart-shaped leaflets make the family easily recognized. The flowers, ¼ inch or more in width, are pale yellow.

Several other species of the genus bloom throughout the warm months and will come in for attention of the student of fall flowers. *O. corniculata* (L.) is quite similar to the above but is creeping. RED-LEAVED WOOD-SORREL *O. europaea cymosa* Small, attracts attention by being almost wholly purplish-red. Its flowers, too, are light yellow.

67b Leaves pinnately-compound with 5 or more leaflets; calyx 5-lobed; plants without sour sap. 68

68a Fruit top-shaped, bristly; leaflets toothed, one of them terminal; plant not sensitive to touch. 69

68b Fruit a pod, not bristly; leaflets entire, no terminal one; plants more or less sensitive (drooping leaves, etc.) to touch. 70

69a Leaves without glandular dots beneath; compound leaves usually with but one pair of tiny leaf-segments between each larger pair of leaflets, as pictured (a). Fig. 152.

SOFT AGRIMONY *Agrimonia pubescens* Wallr.

Figure 152

This plant is tuberous-rooted and grows to a height of 1½ to 6 feet. There are 5 to 11 fairly large leaflets with a single pair of tiny leaflets alternating between the larger ones. The flowers are yellow, about ¼ inch broad and are borne in loose racemes. It is fairly common in dry woods.

Several other species of the genus are also late bloomers.

69b Leaves glandular-dotted beneath; interposed leaf-segments several instead of but one pair as in *mollis.* **Fig. 153.**

BRITTON'S AGRIMONY *Agrimonia striata* Michx.

This robust plant has a fibrous root system and grows to a height of 2 to 6 feet in roadsides, woods and thickets. The hirsuit-pubescent compound leaves have 5 to 9 fairly large leaflets, much as in the preceding, but with many tiny segments interspersed between them. The deep-yellow flowers, about ¼ inch across are crowded in long racemes The small dry fruit is covered with hooked bristles.

Figure 153

70a Flowers large (1 to 1½ inches broad), long-pedicelled; stamens 10. Fig. 154.

PARTRIDGE PEA *Cassia fasciculata* Michx.

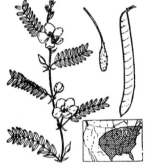

This interesting plant grows to a height of 1 to 2 feet along roadsides and in open woods and fields. There are 20 to 30 leaflets on the feather-like leaves; there is a prominent gland near the base of the petiole. The flowers grow in twos to fours in the axils of the leaves; they are an inch or more across and are bright yellow, sometimes with purple spots on the petals. Six of the stamens have purple anthers while the other four have yellow anthers. The pods are flat and thin and are 1½ to 2½ inches long.

Figure 154

70b Flowers small (1/3 inch or less broad), short-pedicelled; stamens 5. Fig. 155.

WILD SENSITIVE PLANT *Cassia nictitans* L.

This is a smaller but somewhat similar plant to the fore-going. It grows from 6 to 15 inches high and seems to prefer dry soil. The leaves have 14 to 42 leaflets. The yellow flowers are about ¼ inch broad; they have 5 stamens and are borne 1 to 3 in the leaf axils. The pods, 1 to 1½ inches long, are linear, flattened and often pubescent.

Figure 155

71a Stamens more numerous than the corolla lobes.
Fig. 156. 72

Figure 156

71b Stamens the **same** number as the corolla lobes or fewer.
Fig. 157. 88

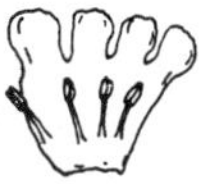

Figure 157

72a Sepals 2, scale-like; petals 4, in 2 sets, the outer 2 spurred at the base (a); a vine. Fig. 158.

CLIMBING FUMITORY *Adlumia fungosa* (Ait.)

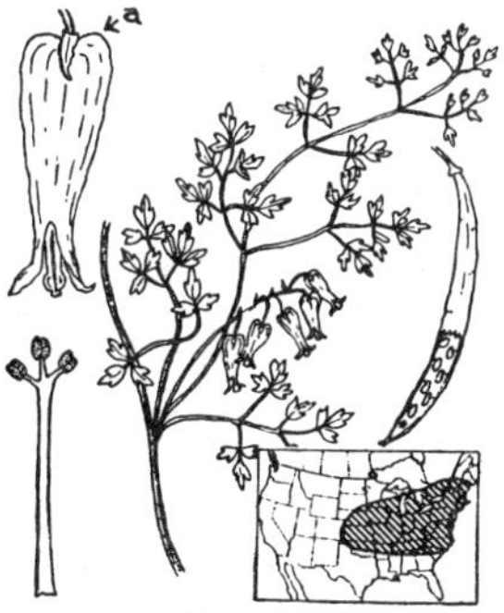

This is a slender climbing vine which is found in woods and banks of streams. The leaves are twice compound. The pink or greenish-white flask-shaped flowers hang suspended from cymes. The fruit is a slender, 2-valved capsule. Mountain Fringe and Fairy Creeper are other common names.

Figure 158

72b Sepals or calyx lobes 4 or 5; petals 3 or 5 (2 lower petals of Leguminosae more or less united). 73

73a Sepals 5, the 2 lateral ones (wings) colored and petal-like; petals 3, somewhat united; ovary 2-celled, 2-seeded. 74

73b Calyx 4 or 5 toothed, sometimes 2-lipped; petals 5, the 2 lower ones (keel) more or less united; ovary one-celled, one to many-seeded; flowers sweet-pea shaped. Fig. 159. 75

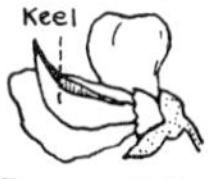

Figure 159

74a At least the lower leaves whorled; wings (lateral sepals) over ⅛ inch long, much exceeding the pod. Fig. 160.

CROSS-LEAVED MILKWORT *Polygala cruciata* L.

Over 400 widely scattered species of this genus are known. The species here pictured is an erect, glabrous annual sometimes reaching a height of a foot or more. The narrow leaves, ½ to 1½ inches long, are usually in whorls of four. The flowers are purple, white or greenish and grow in rather compact terminal heads.

FIELD MILKWORT *P. viridescens* L. appears similar but has alternate leaves. It grows in fields and meadows over much of our region.

Figure 160

74b Leaves all alternate; wings less than ⅛ inch long, only slightly exceeding the pod. Fig. 161.

MARYLAND MILKWORT *Polygala mariana* Mill.

This 6 to 15 inch annual is often much branched and is glabrous. The alternating leaves are less than an inch long; the lower ones are frequently spatulate. The flowers are rose-purple and are borne in rounded terminal heads.

CURTISS' MILKWORT *P. curtissii* Gray and NUTTALL'S MILKWORT *P. nuttallii* T. & G. are both similar plants but considerably smaller and with more elongate heads. The flowers are purple in the first but greenish or yellowish-purple in the latter.

Figure 161

75a Leaves simple (a); pod inflated. Fig. 162.

RATTLE-BOX *Crotalaria sagittalis* L.

This dryland plant with maximum height of about a foot is also known as Loco-weed or Wild Pea. The entire plant is covered with a dense pubescence; the leaves are practically sessile and are from 1 to 2½ inches long. The pale yellow flowers about ½ inch long are borne in racemes of 2 to 4. The inflated pods, about 1 inch long, becoming black, contain the shining seeds and give the common name.

Figure 162

75b Leaves compound (with 3 or more leaflets per leaf). Fig. 163. 76

Figure 163

76a Leaflets usually 25 to 55, somewhat sensitive when touched; flowers yellowish to reddish-yellow. Fig. 164.

SENSITIVE JOINT VETCH *Aeschynomene virginica* (L.)

This erect annual grows to a height of 2 to 5 feet and is found on low ground, river-banks and swamps. The feathery leaves becoming 2 inches or more in length have 25 to more than 50 leaflets. The flowers are nearly ½ inch long; the petals are reddish-yellow and show prominent veins. The pods are divided into several valves.

Figure 164

76b Leaflets usually 3 to 7, not sensitive; flowers mostly purplish, pink, or white. 77

77a Plants vine-like, twining or trailing. 78

77b Plants erect. 82

78a Leaflets 5 to 7 (rarely 3). Fig. 165.

GROUNDNUT *Apios americana* Medic.

This slender plant grows in damp ground or climbs on other plants to a length of a few feet. It produces several tubers. The leaves are rather large and have 5 to 7 leaflets. The flowers are about ½ inch long, brownish-purple, fragrant and borne in numerous flowered racemes. The many-seeded bean up to 4 inches or more in length has been used for food.

Figure 165

78b Leaflets 3. 79

65

79a (a, b, c) Fruit a loment (a), separating crosswise into 3 or more one-seeded sections; leaflets almost round, over one inch long. Fig. 166.
PROSTRATE TICK-TREFOIL *Desmodium rotundifolium* (Michx.)

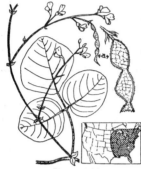

This more or less pubescent trailer grows to a length of 3 to 6 feet. The leaves have 3 leaflets and a pair of ovate stipules. The flowers are purple about 1/3 inch long and borne in open, terminal panicles. The fruit is a flattened pod which is divided into several one-seeded packets. (loment). These parts separate from each other readily when mature and stick to passing animals as an aid in dispersal.

Figure 166

79b Fruit a loment of usually one section about ¼ inch long (sometimes 2 sections); leaflets oval, less than one inch long. Fig. 167.
TRAILING BUSH CLOVER *Lespedeza procumbens* (Michx.)

This heavily pubescent trailer produces vines up to 2 or 3 feet long. the tri-foliate leaves have short petioles. The small flowers are pinkish- or violet-purple. The pods are oval, single seeded and less than ¼ inch long. It overgrows dry banks and is found along roadsides.

Figure 167

79c Fruit a pod, one to 4 inches long; leaflets mostly ovate to ovate-lanceolate, over one inch long. 80

80a Style with very few hairs or none, very slightly curved; keel (2 lower petals) not twisted. Fig. 168.

HOG-PEANUT *Amphicarpa bracteata* (L.)

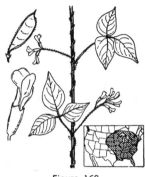

Figure 168

This is a climbing vine which grows in moist thickets and damp woods. The three leaflets are ovate and acute at their tip; the stipules are elongate and usually small. The flowers are borne in small racemes; they are about ½ inch long and range in color from white to blue and violet. After blooming, the young fruit penetrate the soil, like the peanut and mature the 1 to 2-seeded, inch-long pods under ground.

80b Style bearded, strongly curved; keel spirally coiled or strongly curved. 81

81a Keel spirally coiled; flowers in long loose racemes. Fig. 169.

WILD BEAN *Phaseolus polystachios* (L.)

Figure 169

This vine trails to considerable length over other plants. The lanceolate stipules fall early; the three leaflets are ovate with acuminate tip and are 2 to 4 inches long. The purple flowers measure about 1/3 inch. The pods are flat, somewhat curved and may attain a length of 2 inches or more. The seeds are chocolate colored.

81b Keel curved inward, not spirally coiled; flowers in umbel-like clusters. Fig. 170.

TRAILING WILD BEAN *Strophostyles helvola* (L.)

Figure 170

Look in sandy soil for this trailing legume which may attain a length of 10 feet. The entire plant, root and all, is an annual. The leaflets are 1 to 2 inches long and are often three lobed. The sessile flowers, nearly ½ inch long, are borne in compact spikes of 3 to 10. The flowers are purple or greenish-purple. The slender, 2 to 3 inch long pods contain several pubescent seeds.

82a At least the lower leaves with 5 leaflets, glandular-dotted; fruit a one-seeded pod. Fig. 171.

MANY-FLOWERED PSORALEA *Psoralea tenuiflora floribunda* (Nutt.)

Figure 171

Growing 1 to 4 feet high, this densely-hairy plant produces 3 to 7 leaflets on its leaves. The stipules are short and narrow. It is a prolific bloomer; the flowers are 1/3 inch long and variable in color, white, pink or bluish. The light brown pod is glandular specked and bears one, somewhat flattened seed. It is a prairie plant.

82b Leaves 3-foliate, not glandular-dotted; fruit a loment (separating crosswise into one-seeded, veined sections). Fig. 172. 83

Figure 172

83a Loment of several sections; stipules present. Fig. 173a. 84

Figure 173

83b Loment of one to 2 sections (usually one); no stipules. 86

84a Loment not constricted on the upper margin, deeply constriicted below; leaflets oval to ovate; flowering stem (peduncle) usually leafless. Fig. 174.

NAKED-FLOWERED TICK-TREFOIL *Desmodium nudiflorum* (L.)

Figure 174

The members of this genus are characterized by their peculiarly scalloped and flattened fruit pod. Each "scallop" contains a single seed carefully put up for distribution and is usually equipped to adhere to passing animals.

The panicle arises from the base of this species instead of being terminal as in the others. The plant is trifoliate, grows about 3 feet high and has rose-purple flowers about ¼ inch long. It is widely distributed and grows in dry woods.

84b Loment constricted on both margins; leaflets oblong to linear-lanceolate; peduncle leafy. 85

85a Loment distinctly long-stalked in the calyx; plant essentially glabrous; flowers few, about ¼ inch long. Fig. 175.

PANICLED TICK-TREFOIL *Desmodium paniculatum* (L.)

Figure 175

This species arises to a height of 2 to 4 feet, usually with smooth stems. The leaflets are 1 to 2 inches long and lanceolate, often with obtuse tips. The purple flowers measure ¼ inch and produce 4 to 6 jointed pods about an inch in length. It is found in dry soil and in the woods.

85b Loment sessile in the calyx or nearly so; plant hairy, at least on the stem; flowers many, about ½ inch long. Fig. 176.
SHOWY TICK-TREFOIL *Desmodium canadense* (L.)

Figure 176

This sturdy species grows to a height of 3 to 8 feet and produces its flowers in showy terminal panicles. The stipules are lanceolate-linear and the stems pubescent. The conspicuous purple or bluish flowers, more than ½ inch long, are crowded in the panicle. The 3 to 5 jointed fruit becomes about an inch in length.

86a Flowers purplish; calyx much shorter than the pod. Fig. 177a.
STUVE'S BUSH-CLOVER *Lespedeza stuevei* Nutt.

Figure 177

Usually a simple, densely-velvety plant (2-4 feet high) with a few branches, many leaves, and crowded clusters of violet-purple flowers, each about ¼ inch or less in length. The beaked, oval pod is densely-pubescent. Found in dry or sandy soil of rocky shores and woods.

WANDLIKE BUSH CLOVER *Lespedeza intermedia* (S. Wats.) Fig. 177b. is a similar species but is glabrous or only slightly pubescent. The flowers are crowded at the top of the plant. Blooms in August and September in dry soil.

86b Flowers whitish or yellowish; calyx nearly as long or longer than the pod. 87

87a Peduncles mostly longer than the leaves; calyx and pod about equal. Fig. 178.   **HAIRY BUSH-CLOVER** *Lespedeza hirta* (L.)

A rather stiff stout densely hairy plant (2-5 feet high) simple or with few branches. The yellowish-white flowers (about ¼ inch long) are crowded into cylindrical clusters. Often the standard (upper petal) has a purple spot near its base. Found blooming from August to October in dry woods and fields.

Frequently in this genus the flowers are of two kinds intermixed: one with petals but sterile, the other without petals, but producing seed.

Figure 178

87b Peduncles shorter than the leaves; calyx much longer than the pod. Fig. 179.

ROUND-HEADED BUSH-CLOVER *Lespedeza capitata* Michx.

This plant standing stiffly erect to a height of 2 to 5 feet, is covered with a soft silvery pubescence. The leaflets are more than an inch long and are acute at each end. The flowers, measuring about ¼ inch, are yellowish-white marked with purple. The small oval pod produces a single seed. The plant turns a chocolate brown after frost and stands out conspicuously.

Figure 179

88a Ovary superior (above the calyx). Fig. 180......89

Figure 180

88b Ovary inferior (below the calyx). Fig. 181......158

Figure 181

89a Corolla regular (lobes all alike). Fig. 182. 90

Figure 182

89b Corolla irregular (lobes unlike). Fig. 183. *(Verbena, Isanthus, Mentha, Lycopus, Verbascum* sometimes with corolla lobes only slightly different). 110

Figure 183

90a Ovaries 2, often with the stigmas united; a 5-parted crown (corona) between the corolla and the stamens (Fig. 184); plants with milky juice. 91

Figure 184

90b Ovary one; flower without a crown; plants without milky juice. 93

91a Stem twining; leaves ovate with prominent heart-shaped base. Fig. 185. SAND VINE *Ampelamus albidus* (Nutt.)

The novice is sometimes very much surprised to find a vining milkweed; there are a number of species of which this is one. The deeply cordate leaves, 3 to 7 inches long, have slender petioles and are opposite. The small whitish flowers are borne in dense cymes from the leaf axils. The fruit is a smooth follicle 4 to 6 inches long; the flat seeds are each attached to a tuft of long silken hairs for wind dispersal as with the other milkweeds.

Figure 185

91b Stem erect; leaves linear, lanceolate or oblong-lanceolate, rarely heart-shaped at base. 92

92a Flowers whitish; leaves linear, whorled in 3's to 7's. Fig. 186.
WHORLED MILKWEED *Asclepias verticillata* L.

This slender little milkweed abounds in dry fields; it grows from 1 to 2 feet high. The linear leaves are borne in whorls of 3 to 7 and are an inch or two in length. The flowers are borne in rather dense umbels; they are greenish-white. The slender follicles, 2 to 3 inches long, stand erect.

Figure 186

92b Flowers rose to reddish-purple; leaves lanceolate to oblong-lanceolate, usually opposite. Fig. 187.

SWAMP MILKWEED *Asclepias incarnata* L.

In swamps and other low wet places this beautiful milkweed may often be found in abundance. It has a height of 2 to 4 feet. Its leaves are up to 6 inches long and are lanceolate. The flowers are rose-purple or reddish and are often marked with white. The follicles are held erect and may be 3 inches or more in length.

SULLIVANT'S MILKWEED *A. sullivantii* Engl. is a stout broad-leaved species that is also a fall bloomer. It is wholly glabrous; the rather large flowers are purplish-red.

Figure 187

93a Leaves basal; petals dry and membranous; flowers small, many in dense spikes. Fig. 188.

RIB GRASS *Plantago lanceolata* L.

This is an all-too-common weed which has been permitted to slip in from Europe. The 3 to 12 inch long leaves are lanceolate and have 3 to 7 prominent nerves. The somewhat dry scaly whitish flowers are borne in short compact spikes. The flowers are perfect; the fruit is 2-seeded. The seeds are difficult to separate from those of red clover, which results in this weed often being abundant in red clover fields.

Figure 188

93b Leaves alternate or opposite; petals not dry and membranous; flowers medium to large, not in dense spikes. **94**

94a Leaves alternate; fruit a berry. Fig. 189. ....**95**

Figure 189

94b Leaves opposite (reduced to scales in *Bartonia* and sometimes alternate); fruit a capsule. Fig. 190. ...**98**

Figure 190

95a Calyx not changed in fruit; corolla white, the lobes longer than the tube; anthers united into a cone. Fig. 191.

BLACK NIGHTSHADE *Solanum nigrum* L.

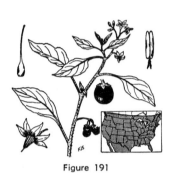

Figure 191

This herbaceous annual weed grows to a height of 1 to 2½ feet and is found in a wide variety of growing situations. The stems and leaves often have a tinting of purple. The leaves are 1 to 3 inches long. The petals are white and the stamens united to project from the center of the flower as is characteristic of this family, Solanaceae, are bright yellow. The fruit is a globular berry about ¼ inch in diameter which changes from green to black at maturity.

Seeds of a cultivated variety which produces larger fruit may be found in the market under the names, Garden Huckleberry, Wonderberry, etc. Some seem to like 'em but they are thought quite inferior by others.

95b Calyx later inflated and enclosing the berry; corolla yellow, the lobes much shorter than the tube; anthers separate. 96

96a Pubescence dense, viscid or glandular (sticky); leaves broadly cordate. Fig. 192.

CLAMMY GROUND CHERRY *Physalis heterophylla* Nees.

Figure 192

This much-spreading, somewhat-decumbent, glandular-villous perennial may attain a height of 3 feet. The rather large leaves are usually coarse toothed. The flowers, nearly an inch in diameter are borne singly in the axils and are yellow with a purple or brownish center. The berry is globular; it is surrounded by the inflated sack-like calyx and becomes yellow at ripening and the calyx becomes dry and husk-like. The fruit of this and other species is often used for making preserves, etc.

96b Pubescence sparse, rarely viscid or glandular; leaves ovate, ovate-lanceolate, or lanceolate. 97

**97a Leaves thick, lanceolate or oblanceolate, the lower ones often
spatulate; fruiting calyx scarcely sunken at the base. Fig. 193.
PRAIRIE GROUND CHERRY** *Physalis lanceolata* **Michx.**

This perennial of 1 foot height, spreads
by a creeping rootstalk. It is a plant of
the prairies. The leaves are lanceolate or
occasionally spatulate. The flowers, about
2/3 inch across are dull yellow with a
brownish center. The calyx surrounding
the fruit is smooth and in contrast to many
of the other ground cherries is not sunk-
en at the base; the berry becomes yellow
or greenish-yellow when mature.

Figure 193

**97b Leaves thin, ovate-lanceolate; fruiting calyx deeply sunken at the
base. Fig. 194.
VIRGINIA GROUND CHERRY** *Physalis virginiana* **Mill.**

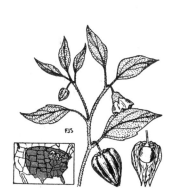

A somewhat fleshy perennial growing from a thickened rootstalk. The stem
has a covering of appressed hairs; the
leaves taper at both ends and are up
to 2½ inches long, sometimes dentate
or may be entire, and are frequently
yellowish-green. The flowers are purplish spotted on a sulphur-yellow corolla. The fruiting calyx is 5-angled and
much sunken at its base; the fruit becomes reddish.

Some species of ground cherries have
blackish or deep purple berries. Husk-
tomato is a term applied to some cultivated species.

Figure 194

98a Ovary 3-celled; flowers many in a compact cymose panicle.
Fig. 195.   GARDEN PHLOX *Phlox paniculata* L.

Though a native plant, this species is widely cultivated as an ornamental and as such is seen in numerous shades of color. It is a perennial attaining a height of some 3 feet or more. The opposite leaves are 2 to 6 inches long. The flowers have short pedicels and are crowded in broad paniculate cymes and range from purple and reddish to white.

Figure 195

98b Ovary one-celled; flowers mostly one to several, if numerous, not in cymose panicles. 99

99a Leaves reduced to scales; flowers yellowish-white, ¼ inch or less in length. Fig. 196a.
YELLOW BARTONIA *Bartonia virginica* (L.)

Sometimes known as Screw-stem, this odd little plant grows to a height of 5 to 15 inches in damp places. The leaves are opposite but have been reduced to tiny scales. The flowers are yellowish-white or greenish and less than ¼ inch long. The tiny capsule is compressed, somewhat 4-sided and filled with minute seeds.

BRANCHED BARTONIA *B. paniculata* (Michx.) 196b is a slender plant growing in wet soil to a height of a foot or more. Its range is more restricted than *virginica*. The flowers are greenish or yellowish white with yellow anthers. These two belong to the Gentian family.

Figure 196

99b Leaves normal; flowers mostly blue, pink, or white (one species yellowish) ½ to 2 inches in length. 100

100a Style thread-like; corolla rose-colored or white, rotate (flat and circular). 101

100b Style none or short and thick; corolla blue, (occasionally white or yellowish); bell-shaped or tube-shaped. 102

101a Flowers 4 to 7 parted (usually 4 to 5 parted), ¾ to 1½ inches broad. Fig. 197.   SEA PINK *Sabatia stellaris* Pursh.

This plant belongs to the brackish meadows of the Atlantic coast. It is much branched and stands 6 to 20 inches high. The sessile leaves are about 2 inches long and are almost linear. The showy flowers are up to 1½ inches across and are pink or white with a yellow center which is bordered with red.

Figure 197

101b Flowers 8 to 12 parted, 1¼ to 2¼ inches broad. Fig. 198.
            LARGE MARSH PINK *Sabatia dodecandra* (L.)

This plant grows on the margins of ponds and salt-marshes. The basal leaves are spatulate and up to 3 inches long; the upper stem leaves are opposite and linear or lanceolate. It stands from a foot to 2 feet high. The rather few flowers are 2 inches or more broad and are pink (rarely white) with 8 to 12 lobes to the corolla. The fruit is a small globular capsule.

Figure 198

102a Corolla with plaits (toothed processes) between the lobes. Fig. 199. 105

Figure 199

102b Corolla without plaits between the lobes. Fig. 200. 103

Figure 200

103a Corolla lobes entire, triangular; flowers less than one inch long.
Fig. 201.   STIFF GENTIAN *Gentiana quinquefolia* L.

Figure 201

This annual "Ague-weed" may attain a height of over 2 feet. The basal leaves are spatulate but those higher on the stem are clasping and often somewhat cordate at the base and are rather prominently 3 to 7 nerved. The flowers are blue or purplish-blue and a little less than an inch long. They are usually in terminal clusters of 3 to 7 but others may be found in the axils. It grows in limy soil or rich woods.

103b Corolla lobes fringed or toothed, rounded; flowers 1½ to 2 inches long. 104

104a Leaves (at least the upper ones) linear or linear-lanceolate; tapering at the base. Fig. 202.
          SMALLER FRINGED GENTIAN *Gentiana procera* Holm.

Figure 202

This sparingly branched annual has a height of 3 to 15 inches. Its lower leaves are obtuse spatulate while the upper stem leaves are linear and around 2 inches long. The flowers are usually 4-parted, bright blue, with the corolla lobes rather deeply fringed over the entire margin. The flowers are about 1½ inches high and are borne singly on long erect peduncles with 1 to 5 or 6 for each plant. It grows in wet regions.

104b Leaves lanceolate to oblong-lanceolate, base rounded or heart-shaped. Fig. 203.

FRINGED GENTIAN *Gentiana crinita* Froel.

Figure 203

It may be either an annual or a biennial and is noticeably larger than the preceding, sometimes reaching a height of 3 feet. The upper leaves are oblong lanceolate and about 2 inches long. The bright blue flowers are 2 inches high and terminal and solitary. The long fringe is confined to the ends of the corolla lobes. There are occasional plants which bear white flowers. The fruit is a spindle-shaped capsule.

105a Flowers borne singly on a distinct stem; leaves linear. Fig. 204.

ONE-FLOWERED GENTIAN *Gentiana autumnalis porphyrio* J. F. Gmel.

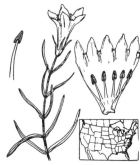

Figure 204

A glabrous perennial standing 5 to 15 inches high. The opposite leaves are nearly linear and 1 to 2 inches long. The solitary terminal flower stands about 2 inches high; it is bright blue and is sometimes marked within with brownish. The fruit is a small capsule containing many fine seeds. It grows in acid bogs and in pinelands.

105b Flowers clustered, usually sessile; leaves mostly lanceolate to ovate-lanceolate. **106**

106a Anthers separate (at least at maturity); corolla bell-shaped or funnel-form, open, the lobes spreading. **107**

106b Anthers united in a tube or ring; corolla cylindric, oblong, or club shaped, its lobes erect or touching. **108**

107a Plaits unequally lobed; corolla bell-shaped funnel-form.
Fig. 205.   **DOWNY GENTIAN** *Gentiana puberula* **Michx.**

This prairie member of the Gentian Family is widely distributed. It may grow to a height of a foot or more and has narrow lanceolate leaves, 1 to 3 inches long which are pale on their under side. A few rose-purple, sessile flowers are clustered in the top-most axils. They are 1½ to 2 inches long. The capsule is spindle-shaped and becomes nearly an inch long.

Figure 205

107b Plaits equally lobed; corolla narrowly funnel-form. Fig. 206.
          OBLONG-LEAVED GENTIAN *Gentiana affinis* **Griseb.**

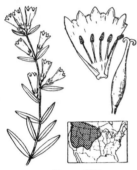

A western perennial growing to a height of a foot or more enters a part of our area. Like many others of the genus it prefers damp soil. The leaves average about an inch in length. The flowers stand about 1 inch high and are blue or purplish; the corolla is 2-cleft and toothed as pictured.

Figure 206

108a Corolla yellowish-white, greenish-white, or purplish-green; leaf margins smooth or nearly so. Fig. 207.
          YELLOWISH GENTIAN *Gentiana flavida* **Gray.**

So many of the gentians are a bright blue that it is easy to think of all gentians being that color; here is one that differs from the others in having its flowers yellowish-white or sometimes greenish-white. The plant stands from 1 to 3 feet high with pointed ovate, usually clasping leaves, 2 to 4 inches long. The flowers are 1½ to 2 inches long and are borne in crowded clusters at the top of the plant. The seeds are winged.

Figure 207

108b Corolla blue; leaf margins rough. 109

109a Corolla lobes small and inconspicuous, much exceeded by the broad-tipped plaits; capsule ¾ to one inch long. Fig. 208.
CLOSED GENTIAN *Gentiana andrewsii* Griseb.

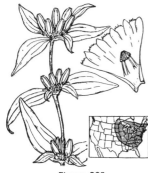

Figure 208

Growing 1 to 2 feet high in meadows, prairies, swamps and damp woods, this plant has pointed lanceolate leaves 2 to 4 inches long. The corolla is blue or purplish and from 1 to 1½ inches long; there are occasional white flowers. The anthers are fused together. The small capsule is spindle-shaped. It is sometimes known as Bottle or Barrel Gentian.

109b Corolla lobes and narrow plaits about the same length; capsule about ½ inch long. Fig. 209.
SOAPWORT GENTIAN *Gentiana saponaria* L.

Figure 209

This, still another of the closed gentians stands 1 to 2 feet or more in height. The glabrous, ovate-lanceolate leaves measure 1 to 3 inches. The flowers are blue or purplish-blue and are about 1½ inches high. The fruit is a capsule less than an inch in length. It seems to prefer acid soil.

110a Leaves none or reduced to scales. 111

110b Leaves present, normal. 112

111a Aquatic plant with underwater stems bearing many tiny bladders;
stamens 2; leaves none. Fig. 210.

PURPLE BLADDERWORT *Utricularia purpurea* Walt.

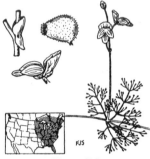

Figure 210

This is a submerged leafless aquatic
annual, but the branches are whorled
and very much compounded. The bladders which are characteristic of all the
bladderworts are at the ends of the
stems and smaller than in many of the
other species. The scapes are several
inches long to hold the 2 to 4 flowers
above water. The corolla is reddish-
purple, the lower lip being marked
with a yellow spot. The numerous tiny
seeds are in a small capsule.

111b Purplish or yellowish plant parasitic on beech roots; stamens 4;
leaves reduced to scales. Fig. 211.

BEECH-DROPS *Epifagus virginiana* (L.)

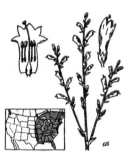

Figure 211

The members of this Orobanchaceae Family live a parasitic life and accordingly do
not need and do not have chlorophyll. This
species which is found growing under beech
trees as parasites of their roots attains a
height of ½ to 2 feet. It has a few small
scaly remnants of leaves near the base.
There are two types of flowers, those which
do not open (cleistogamous) standing lower
on the raceme and normal flowers above.
The entire plant is pale yellowish or purplish, the flowers usually being lighter colored than the other parts.

112a Fruit of 4 (or fewer) nutlets; ovules one in each of the 4
cells (*Echium* appears 4-celled although sometimes it is
2-celled). Fig. 212. 113

Figure 212

112b Fruit a capsule; ovules 2 to many in the 1, 2 or 5 cells
(*Proboscidea* sometimes falsely 2-4 celled). Fig. 213. 140

Figure 213

113a Ovary 4-lobed or 4-parted; style from between the lobes (Fig. 214); plants usually square-stemmed and often with aromatic foliage *(Echium* not square-stemmed nor aromatic). 114

Figure 214

113b Ovary not lobed; style from the top of the ovary (Fig. 215); foliage not aromatic. 137

Figure 215

114a Leaves alternate. Fig. 216.

VIPER'S BUGLOSS *Echium vulgare* L.

This biennial is clothed with bristly hairs and stands at a height of 1 to 2 feet. The linear-lanceolate leaves are often sessile and are from 2 to 6 inches long. The bright blue flowers are nearly an inch long; they are sometimes purplish-violet and since the flower buds are pink the whole effect is a variegated one. The fruit consists of 4 nutlets. Other names are Blueweed and Blue-devil.

Figure 216

114b Leaves opposite. Fig. 217. (Mint Family) 115

Figure 217

115a Ovary of 4 united carpels, merely 4-lobed; nutlets attached by their sides. 116

115b Ovary of 4 distinct or nearly-distinct carpels; nutlets attached by their bases. 117

116a Calyx nearly regular; corolla nearly regular; stamens somewhat exserted. Fig. 218.

FALSE PENNYROYAL *Isanthus brachiatus* (L.)

This is an annual herb which grows in sandy soil to a maximum height of about a foot and a half. The somewhat lanceolate leaves are 3-nerved, pointed at each end and usually entire; they have a length of 1 to 2 inches. The flowers are borne 1 to 3 in axillary cymes and are only ¼ inch long; their color is blue.

Figure 218

116b Calyx very irregular, 2-lipped; corolla 2-lipped; stamens long-exserted. Fig. 219. BLUE CURLS *Trichostema dichotomum* (L.)

This annual member of the Mint Family stands at a height of ½ to 2 feet. The leaves are densely covered with a coat of sticky pubescence. They are from 1 to 3 inches long. The blue or sometimes white flowers are about ½ inch long and are borne in leafy panicles; the anthers are blue or violet. The ovary is deeply 4-lobed. It grows in dry fields.

Figure 219

117a Calyx 2-lipped, not toothed; calyx with a protuberance on the upper side (a). Fig. 220.

MAD-DOG SKULLCAP *Scutellaria lateriflora* L.

A perennial growing from a slender rootstalk to a height of 6 to 30 inches with coarsely serrate leaves 1 to 3 inches long. The 1-to-several flowered leafy racemes are terminal. The flowers are blue, or in some plants nearly white and measure about 1/3 inch in length. The plant grows in wet places.

Figure 220

84

117b Calyx 2-lipped or nearly regular, 3 to 5-toothed; no protuberance on the calyx. 118

118a Corolla conspicuously 2-lipped, lips unlike, the upper lip concave. Fig. 221. 119

Figure 221

118b Corolla nearly regular, if 2-lipped, upper lip flat or only slightly concave. Fig. 222. 126

Figure 222

119a Anther-bearing stamens 2. 120

119b Anther-bearing stamens 4. 121

120a Corolla scarlet; flower cluster usually solitary, terminal. Fig. 223.   OSWEGO TEA *Monarda didyma* L.

Figure 223

This rather sturdy-growing 2 to 3 foot plant is very showy when its large scarlet heads are in bloom. It is native to the eastern part of our country but is frequently raised as an ornamental over a much wider range. The ovate-lanceolate leaves are sharply serrate and measure 3 to 6 inches long. The upper leaves and stems are often tinged with bronze or dark red. The conspicuous scarlet flowers with exserted stamens are 1½ inches or more in length.

120b Corolla yellowish with purple spots; flower clusters both axillary and terminal. Fig. 224.

HORSE MINT *Monarda punctata* L.

Figure 224

This dry-field perennial stands 2 to 3 feet high. The lanceolate leaves have small serations or are sometimes entire and are 1 to 3 inches long. The yellowish, purple-spotted flowers 1 inch long are borne in several axillary clusters.

WILD BERGAMOT *M. fistulosa* L. often covers whole hillside pastures and makes a notable display with its terminal heads of lilac or purplish-pink flowers. The flowers are about 1 inch long.

121a Upper (or inner) pair of stamens longer than the lower (or outer) pair. Fig. 225. 122

Figure 225

121b Upper pair of stamens shorter than the lower pair. Fig. 226. 124

Figure 226

122a **Anther-sacs diverging (spread in opposite directions) (a); lower corolla lip purple-spotted. Fig. 227.**

CATNIP *Nepeta cataria* L.

Figure 227

This European mint has become a common weed in much of our region. It is densely pubescent and pale green, the leaves being still lighter on the under side. The flowers are whitish or pale purple with dark dots and are about ½ inch long. The common name likely bears reference to the liking of cats for this rather highly scented plant. It is sometimes put into little cloth bags as "catnip balls" for cats to play with. In an earlier day tea made from the leaves of the plant was a popular remedy for colicky babies.

122b **Anther-sacs parallel or nearly so (Fig. 228); lower corolla lip without spots.** 123

Figure 228

123a **Corolla purplish, much exceeding the calyx. Fig. 229.**
FIGWORT GIANT-HYSSOP *Agastache scrophulariaefolia* (Willd.)

Figure 229

This great mint grows to a height of 6 or 7 feet with heavy 4-angled stems. The leaves are coarsely dentate and are green on both sides. The corolla is purplish and about ½ inch long.

It is a sturdy volunteer in fence-rows and waste land and is found also growing in the woods. The whole plant is rather densely pubescent.

123b Corolla greenish-yellow, slightly exceeding the calyx. Fig. 230.

CATNIP GIANT-HYSSOP *Agastache nepetoides* (L.)

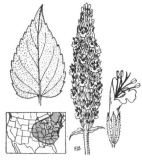

Figure 230

This is a somewhat smaller plant than the preceding species to which it is closely related. The stems are nearly or wholly glabrous. The corolla is about 1/3 inch long and is greenish-yellow, scarcely exceeding the length of the calyx. The nutlets are covered with a minute pubescence.

124a Calyx definitely 2-lipped; floral bracts broadly ovate-orbicular. Fig. 231. HEAL-ALL *Prunella vulgaris* L.

Figure 231

This plant has also been naturalized from Europe, and is frequently seen in waste places though it is not a serious weed. It grows to a height of 15 to 20 inches and has a tendency to be decumbent. The leaves are 1 to 4 inches long. The purple flowers, occasionally white, are borne in elongate terminal spikes which attain a length of 3 to 4 inches in fruit.

124b Calyx not 2-lipped, usually irregular but with the lobes essentially alike; floral bracts lanceolate or upper leaves reduced to narrow bracts. 125

125a Flowers purplish-pink, about one inch long, in a dense, continuous spike; leaves mostly lanceolate. Fig. 232.

DRAGON-HEAD *Physostegia virginiana* (L.)

Here is another native plant that has been brought in and used as an ornamental. It grows to a height of 1 to 3 feet. The oblong-lanceolate, sharply serrate leaves are 2 to 5 inches long. The inch-long rose or pale purple flowers, sometimes marked with white, grow in terminal spikes 4 to 8 inches long and are very showy. The name "Obedient Plant" refers to its staying in whatever position it is put.

Figure 232

125b Flowers purplish, less than ½ inch long, in interrupted spikes; leaves linear. Fig. 233.

HYSSOP HEDGE NETTLE *Stachys hyssopifolia* Michx.

Here we have a smaller perennial growing to a height of 1 to 1½ feet. It is practically glabrous throughout; the leaves are thin, pointed at both ends and have entire margins; they are 1 to 2 inches long. A few to several light purple flowers a little over ½ inch long are borne in interrupted spikes. The ovary is deeply 4-lobed and the style 2-cleft at its top.

Figure 233

127a Anther-bearing stamens 2; corolla pale yellow, lower lip fringed. Fig. 234.   RICH-WEED *Collinsonia canadensis* **L.**

Figure 234

This sturdy plant grows from a hard root to a height of 2 to 5 feet. The rather broad ovate leaves are somewhat thickened and are dentate; they are 5 to 10 inches long. The light yellow flowers are borne in large terminal panicles. The flowers are about ½ inch long and have an odor of lemon. It is found in moist woods.

C. punctata Ell., similar to the above but with the branches glandular pubescent, is widely distributed throughout the South.

127b Anther-bearing stamens 4; corolla purplish or white, lower lip merely 3-lobed. Fig. 235.

BEEFSTEAK-PLANT *Perilla frutescens* **(L.)**

Figure 235

The broad purplish-green leaves, 3 to 6 inches long and nearly that wide have given this plant its name. The leaves have long stems with blades pointed at the base and coarsely dentate. It stands 2 to 3 feet high and bears its small white flowers in a sizeable panicle. The nutlets bear prominent reticulations, the narrow calyx tube becoming much extended to house them as they develop. The crushed plant has a strong odor.

128a Corolla nearly regular, 4 to 5-lobed. Fig. 236. ...129

Figure 236

128b Corolla 2-lipped. Fig. 237. 134

Figure 237

129a Anther-bearing stamens 4; foliage strongly aromatic. 130

129b Anther-bearing stamens 2; foliage but slightly aromatic. 132

130a Flower-clusters all axillary, not in terminal spikes. Fig. 238.
FIELD MINT *Mentha arvensis* L.

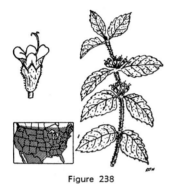

Several well-known mints belong to the genus of this and the two plants which follow. This species with stems up to 2 feet long and somewhat decumbent, has serrate leaves 1 to 2½ inches long. The small lavender flowers are borne in rather dense whorls in the axils of the upper leaves. It has come from Europe; its odor is similar to pennyroyal.

Figure 238

130b Most of the flower-clusters arranged in terminal spike-like panicles. 131

131a Leaves sessile or nearly so; crushed leaves with spearmint odor. Fig. 239. SPEARMINT *Mentha spicata* L.

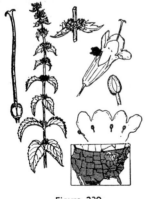

What would the chewing gum factories do if it were not for this mint? It is a glabrous, dark green, rather decumbent perennial with stems nearly 2 feet long. The leaves are lanceolate and sharply serrate. The small pale lavender or whitish flowers grow in terminal spikes, often in interrupted whorls. While it is sometimes cultivated on a large scale, it is often raised in small patches in yards and gardens. It spreads by its underground stems and readily escapes to grow wild. It is European in origin.

Figure 239

90

131b Leaves petioled; crushed leaves with peppermint odor. Fig. 240.
PEPPERMINT *Mentha piperita* **L.**

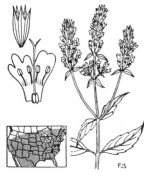

Figure 240

This, too, is a European mint. Much else that has been said for Spearmint could apply here. The flower spikes are much denser and the somewhat larger flowers are a light violet. It grows mostly erect to a possible height of 3 feet. The styles are usually divided into two, but sometimes with three stigmas at their tip. It is raised by the acre in favorable growing areas for commercial use and is the source of one of our best known flavorings.

132a Leaves deeply cut and toothed, at least at the base. Fig. 241.
CUT-LEAVED WATER HOARHOUND *Lycopus americanus* **Muhl.**

Figure 241

This mostly glabrous perennial grows in moist places to a height of 1 to 2 feet. The leaves are 2 to 4 inches long and serrate above the lower ones being deeply cut. The flowers are small, the whitish corolla scarcely extending beyond the calyx.

It should be noted that this is not the hoarhound used in cough remedies. That it is an introduced European plant with rounded, heavily pubescent leaves, COMMON HOARHOUND *Marrubium vulgare* L.. Its white flowers appear in the summer. It is sometimes grown in gardens and makes a persistent weed when it gets out on its own.

132b Leaves merely serrate (toothed). 133

133a Calyx-lobes narrow, very acute, longer than the nutlets. Fig. 242.
   STALKED WATER HOARHOUND *Lycopus rubellus* Moench.

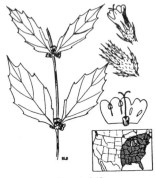

This usually glabrous plant grows to a height of 1 to 3 feet with leaves 2 to 5 inches long. The whitish flowers are about 1/6 inch long and are borne in whorls in the axils. The calyx is about 2/3 as long as the corolla and has triangular subulate teeth. It is found in wet soil.

Figure 242

133b Calyx-lobes ovate, shorter than the nutlets. Fig. 243.
   BUGLE WEED *Lycopus virginicus* L.

A glabrous perennial standing 6 inches to 2 feet high. The ovate to ovate-lanceolate leaves are sharply dentate and are up to 3 inches long; they are frequently tinged with purple. The almost sessile flowers are about ¼ inch long and grow in whorls in the leaf axils.

Figure 243

134a Anther-bearing stamens 2, 2 other stamens often present but much reduced; calyx usually 2-lipped. Fig. 244.
   AMERICAN PENNYROYAL *Hedeoma pulegioides* (L.)

A highly fragrant slender annual growing in dry fields and open woods up to a foot or more in height. The leaves are usually less than an inch long and are covered with a fine pubescence and often purplish on the under side. The flowers are pale lilac with marking of deep purple on the lower lip; they are about 1/5 inch long. The flowers are borne in few-flowered clusters in the axils of the upper leaves.

Figure 244

92

134b Anther-bearing stamens 4; calyx nearly regular (2-lipped in *Pycnanthemum incanum*). 135

135a Anther-sacs divergent (a); leaf-blades less than 1½ inches long. Fig. 245.   **WILD MARJORAM** *Origanum vulgare* L.

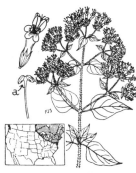

Figure 245

A perennial long horizontal rootstalk carries this herbaceous plant through the winter. It grows to a height of 1 to 2 feet in fields, thickets and roadsides. The leaves are ovate with entire or occasionally shallow toothed margin; the longest ones are about 1½ inches. The numerous flowers are borne in dense terminal clusters; they are about 1/3 inch long and colored pale magenta, lavender or sometimes white.

135b Anther-sacs parallel (Fig. 246); leaf-blades from ½ to 4 inches long. 136

Figure 246

136a (a, b, c) Leaves lanceolate to linear-lanceolate, mostly entire; calyx-lobes equal or nearly so   Fig. 247.

     VIRGINIA MOUNTAIN MINT *Pycnanthemum virginianum* (L.)

Figure 247

This much-branched stiff dense-growing plant is 1 to nearly 3 feet high. The narrow lanceolate leaves are 1 to 2 inches long. The small flowers are in dense terminal clusters and are white with fine specks of purple.

Some 20 North American species of Mountain Mints are known many of which are late in blooming.

136b Leaves narrowly linear to linear-filiform, entire; calyx-lobes equal or nearly so. Fig. 248.

NARROW-LEAVED MOUNTAIN MINT *Pycnanthemum flexuosum* (Walt.)

Figure 248

This species is almost always glabrous. Its stems and leaves are harsh and stiff. The narrow leaves ranges up to 1½ inches in length; the plant grows to a height of 2 feet. The upper lip of the corolla has a small notch while the lower lip is three lobed with the middle lobe considerably narrower than the others. The flowers are whitish.

136c Leaves ovate, elliptic or lanceolate, toothed; calyx somewhat 2-lipped. Fig. 249.

HOARY MOUNTAIN MINT *Pycnanthemum incanum* (L.)

Figure 249

The thin ovate leaves of this plant are usually smooth above but are covered with a white hairy coat on the under side. The species stands from 1½ to 3 feet high with leaves up to 3 inches long and grows in dry places. The flowers are nearly white, about ¼ inch long and are borne in rather crowded terminal clusters.

137a Fruiting spike with fruits densely overlapping. **138**

137b Fruiting spike slender, fruits scattered. **139**

138a Spike stout; corolla about 1/3 inch long; plant densely soft-hairy. Fig. 250. **HOARY VERVAIN** *Verbena stricta* **Vent.**

Figure 250

Pasture fields, roadsides and prairies are colored in late summer and fall with this rather showy plant which grows to a height of 1 to 3 feet. The stems and broad leaves are densely covered with long whitish hairs. Starting at the bottom the succession of flowers moves upward on the long spikes, until some of them may eventually become a foot long. The flowers are 1/3 inch or more broad and more showy than many other members of the genus. They are usually a purplish-blue but are sometimes pink and an occasional plant has pure white flowers.

138b Spike slender; corolla about 1/6 inch long; plant rough-hairy or nearly glabrous. Fig. 251.

BLUE VERVAIN *Verbena hastata* **L.**

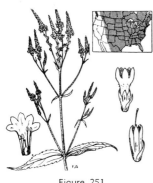

Figure 251

This is a loose-growing tall harsh plant standing 3 to 7 feet high. The leaves, noticeably rough to the touch, are 2 to 5 inches long. The spikes are slender and compact; the small flowers are blue with rather rarely pale pink or white ones. The fruit consists of 4 small nutlets. It is a common pasture, barnyard and waste land weed.

95

139a Corolla white; leaves toothed, not pinnately cleft. Fig. 252.
NETTLE-LEAVED VERVAIN *Verbena urticifolia* L.

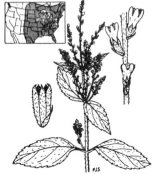

Both the common and scientific names say that this plant has leaves like the nettles, and that is true. In habits of growth it resembles the Blue Vervain but does not grow quite so rank so that 5 feet marks a tall plant. The whole plant is usually pubescent; the leaves are up to 5 inches long; the spikes are very slender and the tiny flowers a clear white.

Figure 252

139b Corolla blue or purplish; leaves once or twice pinnately cleft.
Fig. 253. **EUROPEAN VERVAIN** *Verbena officinalis* L.

This introduced annual has a 4-sided stem, is nearly or quite glabrous and stands 1 to 3 feet high. The leaves have a minute pubescence; some of them are deeply cut and are 1 to 3 inches long. The spikes are usually numerous with the tiny flowers rather scattered. The corolla is purplish or white.

Figure 253

140a Sepals 3, the posterior one large, petal-like, spurred (Fig. 254); capsule 5-celled; anther-bearing stamens 5. 141

Figure 254

140b Calyx 4 to 5-toothed or divided, not spurred (corolla spurred in *Linaria*); capsule one or 2-celled (or falsely 4-celled); anther-bearing stamens 2 or 4 (5 in *Verbascum*). 142

141a Flowers orange; spur long, sharply incurved. Fig. 255.
SPOTTED TOUCH-ME-NOT *Impatiens capensis* Meerb.

Figure 255

This 2 to 5 foot, much-branched and spreading plant is very succulent and rather translucent. It grows in wet rich soil often in luxuriant abundance. The thin ovate leaves may be 3 inches long and are whitish beneath. The orange-yellow flowers are mottled with reddish-brown and are borne in groups of 3 or 4. The fruit of this and the following species is covered with five longitudinal valves which upon separating snap into a coiled position throwing the rather large seeds to some distance. When ripened, the slightest touch to the fruit will precipitate this action, hence the common and generic names.

141b Flowers yellow; spur short, spreading. Fig. 256.
PALE TOUCH-ME-NOT *Impatiens pallida* Nutt.

Figure 256

This plant is much like the preceding but is larger, paler and wider spreading. The flowers are pale yellow with only a few dark dots. Its spindle shaped fruiting body may be an inch or more in length and if gently taken into the hand breaks up, wiggling and twisting like a living animal. Pick one of them carefully and hand to an unsuspecting friend and see the fun.

The sap of both this and the preceding species is sometimes used as a remedy for the irritation caused by Poison Ivy.

142a Placentae parietal (a); capsule, when ripe, 4 to 6 inches long, the anterior end curved and split into 2 sections; entire plant densely sticky-pubescent. Fig. 257.

UNICORN-PLANT *Proboscidea louisiana* (Mill.)

Figure 257

Native to our central region, this curious plant is sometimes raised as a novelty and also for food. The prostrate or assending stems may attain a length of 3 feet. The rounded leaves, often cordate at the base, measure from 3 to 12 inches across and are glandular pubescent. The flowers are 1½ to 2 inches long. They are whitish or yellowish, prettily marked with purple and yellow within. The fruit which becomes 4 to 6 inches long is strongly curved. The fruit while green and tender is sometimes used for pickels, but when ripe and dry it splits part way into halves, each with a vicious prong which has earned it the name "Devil's Claw".

142b Placentae axile (Fig. 258); capsule not over one inch long. 143

Figure 258

143a Anther-bearing stamens 5; leaves alternate. 144

143b Anther-bearing stamens 2 or 4; leaves opposite, whorled, or alternate. 145

144a Plant densely woolly; flowers in a dense, elongate spike. Fig. 259.   COMMON MULLEN *Verbascum thapsus* L.

Figure 259

This well-known weed and waste land plant is of European origin. It is a biennial, producing a large attractive many leaved rosette the first year, then with the energy stored in its fleshy roots it develops a heavy leafy stalk standing 3 to 7 feet high. The entire plant is covered with a thick woolly coat of branching hairs. The leaves are 3 to 12 inches long; the pale yellow flowers, about an inch broad, grow in long dense spikes. The globular capsule contains many tiny seeds.

**144b Plant glabrous or slightly glandular; flowers in a loose raceme.
Fig. 260.** MOTH MULLEN *Verbascum blattaria* L.

Figure 260

Also naturalized from Europe and Asia, it stands 2 to 5 feet high. The leaves are variously shaped, dark green with a glandular pubescence beneath and ranging in length from an inch or two to a foot. The pinkish-white or yellowish flowers, usually a little less than an inch across, are scattered on a terminal raceme, 1 to 2 feet long. The depressed globular capsule measures about ¼ inch.

145a Corolla with a distinct spur at the base (a). Fig. 261.
BUTTER-AND-EGGS *Linaria vulgaris* Hill.

Figure 261

This well-known, 1 to 3 foot plant blooms throughout much of the growing season. It spreads by under-ground root stalks and thus is seen in thick patches. The sessile linear leaves are often ½ to 1½ inches long. The flowers are pale yellow with dark orange spots marking the place on the palate where the bees need to alight to open the corolla.
BLUE-TOADFLAX *L. canadensis* (L.) has violet flowers, about half as long as in the above and on a less compact raceme. The "landing place" in this case is marked white.
COMMON SNAPDRAGON *Antirrhinum majus* L. is larger and differs from the above species in having a sac-like enlargement replacing the long spur.

145b Corolla not spurred at the base. **146**

146a Stamens 5, 4 anther-bearing, the fifth sterile and often rudimentary. **147**

146b Stamens 4 or 2. ....**148**

147a Flowers greenish-purple, about 1/3 inch long, many, in a panicle; sterile stamen a scale on the upper side of the corolla. Fig. 262.   MARYLAND FIGWORT *Scrophularia marilandica* L.

The 4-angled stem of this glabrous or somewhat glandular-pubescent plant grows to a height of 4 to 10 feet. The ovate leaves are serrate, opposite and have long petioles. The odd-shaped flowers, about 1/3 inch long, are greenish-purple and have a conspicuous dark purple sterile stamen.

HARE FIGWORT S. *lanceolata* Pursh, differs from the fore-going in that the sterile stamen is yellowish-green and the corolla is shining on the outside instead of being dull. This plant is somewhat smaller than the other.

Figure 262

147b Flowers mostly white, about one inch long, in a dense, terminal spike; sterile stamen elongate but shorter than the fertile stamens. Fig. 263.   TURTLEHEAD *Chelone glabra* L.

This plant with slender 4-sided stem has a height of 1 to 3 feet and is found along streams and in swamps. The lanceolate leaves having appressed sharp teeth, are 3 to 6 inches long. The flowers are borne in a terminal spike; they are about 1 inch long and are white or occasionally pinkish. The ovoid capsule is about ½ inch long.

RED-TURTLEHEAD C. *obliqua* L. is a similar but somewhat smaller plant and can be distinguished by its red or purplish flowers. It grows in wet places from Va. to Iowa and south to Ark. and Fla.

Figure 263

148a Fertile stamens 2, sometimes with 2 sterile stamens
also present. 149

148b Fertile stamens 4. 151

149a Corolla wheel-shaped, usually with 4 lobes that are quite similar; capsule nearly round, notched at the top (a). Fig. 264.

PURSLANE SPEEDWELL *Veronica peregrina* L.

It is often very abundant in gardens and waste land and flowers from Spring until late Fall. The plant is sometimes a foot high though often much shorter; the narrow leaves are less than an inch long. The very tiny white flowers are borne in the leaf axils; the fruit, a small heart-shaped capsule is more conspicuous.

Several other similar small species of this genus, also bloom until late fall.

Figure 264

149b Corolla tube-shaped, 2-lipped; capsule oval, not notched. **150**

150a Plant glandular-pubescent, at least above; leaves oblong to oblong-lanceolate; corolla whitish. Fig. 265.

CLAMMY HEDGE-HYSSOP *Gratiola virginiana* L.

This erect annual has a height of 3 to 12 inches. The lanceolate leaves are 1 to 2 inches long, narrowed at both ends, sessile and with toothed margin. The flowers are 2-cleft with the lower lip being 3-lobed, their color is white. Most of the mid-summer and fall flowers are cleistogamous.

GOLDEN HEDGE-HYSSOP G. *aurea* Muhl., a somewhat similar species, grows from creeping stems and has entire leaves and bright yellow flowers about 1 inch and ½ inch long respectively. It grows in wet sandy places from Quebec to Florida.

Figure 265

101

150b Plant glabrous; leaves ovate, ovate-oblong, or obovate; corolla purplish. Fig. 266.

LONG-STALKED FALSE PIMPERNEL *Lindernia dubia* (L.)

A much-branched and spreading, slender plant growing to a height of 3 to 10 inches. The leaves are about an inch long, the upper ones with a clasping base. The pale lavender flowers are about 1/3 inch long and are supported by long slender pedicels which arise from the leaf axils. It grows in wet places.

Figure 266

151a Corolla strongly 2-lipped; calyx 2-lobed. Fig. 267.

SWAMP LOUSEWORT *Pedicularis lanceolata* Michx.

Several other members of this genus flower earlier in the year. This wide ranging species grows in swamps and other wet places. It has a height of 1' to 3 feet with leaves measuring 2 to 5 inches. The flowers are not quite an inch long and are yellow. The capsule is about ½ inch long and contains many fine seeds.

Figure 267

151b Corolla slightly irregular; calyx 5-toothed or 5-lobed. 152

152a Corolla yellow, one to 2 inches long. 153

152b Corolla pink, purplish, or white, an inch or less in length..... 155

153a Plant glandular-pubescent; corolla pubescent outside. Fig. 268.
LOUSEWORT FALSE FOXGLOVE *Gerardia pedicularia* **L.**

Figure 268

The False Foxgloves are limited in their places of growth since they are partially parasitic on the roots of other plants and can grow only where their host plant is favorably located for them. This species grows 1 to 4 feet high and is covered with a glandular pubescence. The leaves are 1 to 3 inches long and finely cut, as pictured. The bright yellow flowers are 1½ inches long and about an inch broad. They are pubescent on the outside as is also the capsule.

153b Plant glabrous or pubescent but no glandular hairs; corolla glabrous outside. **154**

154a Leaves pinnatifid or bipinnatifid throughout; capsule glabrous; plant glabrous or minutely pubescent. Fig. 269.
SMOOTH FALSE FOXGLOVE *Gerardia virginica* **(L.)**

Figure 269

This species is a perennial and has a covering of whitish bloom (glaucous) instead of having a hairy covering. The plant attains a height of 3 to 6 feet with leaves 4 to 6 inches long and cut and lobed as pictured. The flowers are yellow, nearly 2 inches long and widely expanded. It seems to prefer dry oak woods.

154b Leaves lanceolate or ovate-lanceolate, the lower ones sometimes pinnatifid; capsule pubescent; plant pubescent. Fig. 270.

DOWNY FALSE FOXGLOVE *Gerardia flava* L.

Figure 270

This plant may often be found in rocky or sandy oak woods where it lives as a partial parasite on the roots of the oak trees. The leaves are pubescent and grayish, with entire margin or lobed; they are usually opposite but are sometimes in whorls of three; they measure 3 to 6 inches. The flowers are bright yellow and about 2 inches long; the capsule is 2/3 inch in length, oblong and pointed at the tip.

155a Leaves lanceolate, some or all of them auricled at the base (a); anthers of the shorter stamens smaller. Fig. 271.

AURICLED GERARDIA *Gerardia auriculata* Michx.

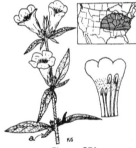

Figure 271

This rough annual has a height of 1 to 2 feet. The leaves are lanceolate and entire except for two narrow elongate lobes at their base and are 1 to 2 inches long. The purple flowers, nearly an inch long are solitary in the upper axils; there are 4 stamens, only 2 of which are functional. The capsule is oblong ½ inch in length.

155b Leaves linear, not auricled at base; anthers alike. 156

156a Flower one to 1½ inches long; pedicels about the same length as the calyx. Fig. 272.

PURPLE GERARDIA *Gerardia purpurea* L.

Figure 272

It is a glabrous annual standing 1 to 2 or more feet high and having very narrow leaves 1 to 1½ inches long. The purple flowers, about an inch long and with broad open mouth are borne in terminal racemes. An occasional plant produces white flowers. The flowers are pubescent on the outside and usually quite hairy within. It grows in moist sandy soil.

156b Flower ½ to ¾ inch long; pedicels 2 or more times longer than
the calyx. 157

157a Petals emarginate (a); leaves revolute (rolled backward from
the margin); flower about ½ inch long. Fig. 273.

TEN-LOBED GERARDIA *Gerardia decemloba* Greene

This slender frail appearing annual grows to a possible height of 2 feet. Each of the five lobes of the corolla is so deeply notched as to make plausible the "Ten-lobed" name. The few leaves are very narrow and less than an inch long. The flowers measure a bit over ½ inch long; they are colored light rose. The fruit is a small oval capsule. It grows in sandy soil.

Figure 273

157b Petals not emarginate; leaves flat; flower ½ to ¾ inch long.
Fig. 274.   SLENDER GERARDIA *Gerardia tenuifolia* Vahl.

Dry woodlands suit this slender glabrous annual; the leaves are thickened but very narrow and from ½ to 1¼ inches long. The flowers are a little over ½ inch long, light purple and marked with spots (occasionally the flowers are white). The calyx tube has but short teeth and in fruit is about half the length of the capsule.

Figure 274

158a Vine-like plant bearing tendrils. 159

158b Plant not tendril-bearing. 160

159a Pistillate flowers mostly solitary; ovary 2 to 3-celled with several ovules; fruit bladdery, usually 4-seeded, opening at the top. Fig. 275. WILD BALSAM APPLE *Echinocystis lobata* (Michx.)

Figure 275

A vigorous growing annual which climbs to a height of 20 or 25 feet. The alternate palmately-compound leaves are 3 to 6 inches across, and are 3 to 7 lobed and deeply cordate. The flowers are about 1/3 inch across and cream colored or white; they are monoecious and are borne in long slender panicles. The thick ovoid fruit becomes about 2 inches long; it is rather thickly covered with long slender spines and contains 2 to 4 large flat seeds.

159b Pistillate flowers clustered; ovary one-celled, one-ovuled; fruit succulent, one-seeded, indehiscent (not opening to discharge seed). Fig. 276. ONE-SEEDED BUR CUCUMBER *Sicyos angulatus* L.

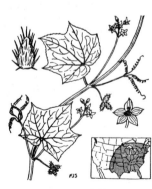

Figure 276

Here is another vining plant belonging to the family Cucurbitaceae. It grows to a length of 18 to 25 feet; the leaves are 3 to 6 inches broad and have 5 distinctly toothed obtuse lobes. The whole plant is more or less viscid-pubescent. The flowers are monoecious; the staminate ones are star-shaped about ½ inch across, yellowish-white, striped with green and borne in racemes. The pistillate flowers grow in heads of 3 to 10. This makes the fruit a cluster of berries each of which is a little less than an inch long and covered with spines.

160a Flowers many, in dense, terminal, spiny heads. Fig. 277.

WILD TEASEL *Dipsacus sylvestris* Huds.

Figure 277

A heavy-set prickly-stemmed biennial growing to a height of 3 to 6 feet. The upper leaves are often perfoliate while others are lanceolate and the lower ones oblong and attaining a length of almost a foot. The flowers are borne in cylindric heads becoming 2 to 4 inches long; the individual flowers, usually less than ½ inch long, are lilac. An involucre of long narrow leaves stands at the base of the head and curves upward. The head when the seeds have ripened is a prickly bur-like body covered with barbed awns. It was once used in carding wool, which explains its introduction from Europe.

160b Flowers axillary, racemed or in spikes, but not in dense spiny heads. 161

161a Leaves opposite; flowers solitary in the leaf axils. Fig. 278.

ROUGH BUTTONWEED *Diodia teres* Walt.

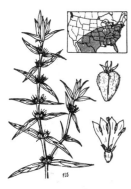

Figure 278

This plant grows in dry or sandy soil. It is often decumbent, but sometimes stands erect to a height of 6 inches to 2 feet. The narrow linear or lanceolate leaves are 1½ inches or less in length. The flowers, ¼ inch long or less, are purplish; usually one in each leaf axil. The small top-shaped fruit gives the common name.

Many plants have several common names and since the same name may be applied to several often widely disrelated species, the chances for confusion is greatly increased. "Buttonweed" is one of these that has been so frequently used that one must also know the scientific name to be sure which plant is meant.

163a Corolla bell-shaped; flowers in a one-sided raceme. Fig. 279.
CREEPING BELLFLOWER *Campanula rapunculoides* L.

Figure 279

This slender, seldom-branched perennial arises from a rootstalk to a height of 1 to 3 feet. The ovate leaves are usually pubescent and toothed; their length is 3 to 6 inches. The bell-shaped blue or purplish flowers 1 to 1½ inches hang from rather long 1-sided racemes. The spherical capsules are suspended and are about 1/3 inch long. We have several native species of Bellflowers, but this and a number of still other species have been introduced from Europe.

163b Corolla flat, wheel-shaped; flowers in a terminal spike. Fig. 280.
TALL BELLFLOWER *Campanula americana* L.

Figure 280

As the name indicates, this is an American species; it is widely distributed and grows in woods and thickets to a height of 2 to 6 feet. The thin, serrate lanceolate leaves measure 3 to 6 inches. The flowers are about an inch broad, open-faced and bright blue, or rarely nearly white. They are borne in long terminal, leafy spikes. The ribbed capsules stand erect to a height of 1/3 inch or more.

164a Leaves mostly basal, hollow, round in cross-section; plant aquatic.
    Fig. 281.   **WATER LOBELIA** *Lobelia dortmanna* L.

Figure 281

This family (Lobeliaceae) of which Lobelia is the largest of some 20 genera has over 600 known species. The flower-stem of this species arises to a height of 1½ feet or less and is leafless except for a few simple scales. The true leaves are narrow, thickened, hollow structures about 1½ inch long which grow under water. The blue flowers are about ½ inch across. It grows at the edge of ponds.

164b Leaves flat, mostly on the stem; plants of moist or dry soil, but not truly aquatic. **165**

165a Flowers bright scarlet (rarely white); corolla one to 1½ inches long. Fig. 282.   **CARDINAL-FLOWER** *Lobelia cardinalis* L.

Figure 282

This species which may grow to a height of 4 feet or more in swamps or other wet places, makes a long-to-be-remembered sight when in full bloom. The rich-green ovate-lanceolate leaves are from 3 to 6 inches long. The flowers measure 1 to 1½ inches in length; the projecting stamens add to the picture; the calyx has 5 linear lobes which persist to surround the globular capsule.

165b Flowers blue or bluish-white; corolla one inch or less in length. **166**

166a Corolla ⅝ to one inch long. **167**

166b Corolla ⅜ inch or less in length. **169**

167a Sepals without basal auricles (ear-shaped appendage). Fig. 283.
SOUTHERN LOBELIA *Lobelia elongata* Small

Here is another swamp-inhabiting lobelia; it is almost wholly glabrous and grows to a possible height of 4 feet. The 2 to 6 inch leaves are thin, ovate and pointed at each end. The bright blue flowers, nearly an inch long, are borne in the terminal raceme. The fruit is a capsule about ¼ inch wide.

Figure 283

167b Sepals with auricles at the base (Fig. 284a). 168

Figure 284

168a Auricles large, acute. Fig. 285.
GREAT LOBELIA *Lobelia siphilitica* L.

"Great" is here well spoken; while its height of 3 feet or less is not outstanding, it more than makes up for that in the size and beauty of its individual flowers. The leaves are 2 to 6 inches long and are often so intermingled with the flowers as to eclipse some of their showyness. The brilliant blue flowers (occasionally white) are an inch or more long and with thicker body than is usual with the lobelias. It grows in creek-beds and other wet places.

Figure 285

168b Auricles small, rounded. Fig. 286.

DOWNY LOBELIA *Lobelia puberula* **Michx.**

This species is somewhat sticky; it grows in low sandy or acid soil to a height of 1 to 3 feet, and is sparingly branched. Its ovate leaves are 1 to 2 inches long. The flowers measure about 2/3 inch long and are bright blue.

Figure 286

169a Leaves oval or obovate; plant pubescent; pod inflated. Fig. 287.

INDIAN-TOBACCO *Lobelia inflata* **L.**

The species name refers to the inflated capsules which make this species rather readily distinguishable. The plant is hirsuit or pubescent and grows to a height of 1 to 3 feet. The oval leaves are up to 2 inches or more in length. The flowers are disappointing in size and color but are daintily formed. They are a pale lavender and measure perhaps a bit over ¼ inch long. The enlarged capsules are more conspicuous than the flowers. Several other plants are also known as "Indian-tobacco" which makes the use of the name confusing.

Figure 287

169b Leaves spatulate to linear-oblong; plant mostly glabrous; pod not inflated. Fig. 288.

BROOK LOBELIA *Lobelia kalmii* **L.**

This glabrous perennial grows in wet places to a height of ½ to 1½ feet. The lower leaves are spatulate and about 2 inches long; the upper ones are nearly linear and shorter. The flowers are borne in loose racemes; they are light blue and less than ½ inch long and have very slender and comparatively long pedicels.

Figure 288

FAMILY COMPOSITAE

1a All the flowers of the head with strap-shaped corollas (ray-flowers); plants usually with milky or bitter juice. Figs. 289 to 313. 2

1b Disk-flowers present; ray-flowers, if present, marginal; juice not milky (milky in *Arechtites*). 20

2a Pappus of scales (a); heads sessile or nearly so, usually blue, showy. Fig. 289.   CHICORY *Cichorium intybus* L.

This European plant has been introduced for use as a substitute or adulterant of coffee, the thickened root being ground and used in that way. The plant has become a common road-side weed in many regions. It grows 1 to 3 feet high and has a stiff, roughened and much branched stem. The stem leaves are clasping; the basal ones, sometimes spatulate and usually lobed, are from 3 to 6 inches long. The heads are an inch or more broad and a beautiful blue (occasionally white).

Figure 289

2b Pappus of bristles (Fig. 290); heads usually on stems. 3

Figure 290

3a Pappus of plumose bristles (a); heads one to several, yellow, on naked or scaly stems. Fig. 291.

FALL DANDELION *Leontodon autumnalis* L.

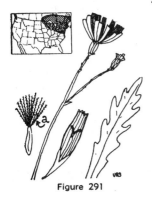

The scape may attain a height of nearly 2 feet. It is scaly but lacks leaves. It arises from a tuft of coarsely toothed leaves 3 to 8 inches in length. The 1 to several yellow heads are an inch or more broad.

ROUGH HAWKBIT *L. leysseri* (Wallr.) is smaller, quite roughly hairy instead of smooth as the preceding and with a solitary head. It has been introduced from Europe and is found around coastal towns.

Figure 291

112

3b Pappus of simple bristles, sometimes rough but not plumose (Fig. 290b); flowers usually many. 4

4a Achenes flattened. Fig. 292. 5

Figure 292

4b Achenes cylindric or prismatic, not flattened. Fig. 293. 11

Figure 293

5a Achenes truncate (ending abruptly) (Fig. 294); flowers yellow, 50 or more in each head; pappus bristles falling away connected. 6

Figure 294

5b Achenes narrowed above into a short or long beak (Fig. 295); flowers yellow, blue or white, 6 to 30 in each head; pappus bristles falling separately. 8

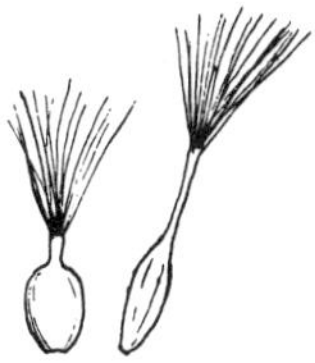

Figure 295

6a Heads about ¾ inch high, bright yellow, showy; involucre gland-ular-bristly. Fig. 296.   FIELD SOW THISTLE Sonchus arvensis L.

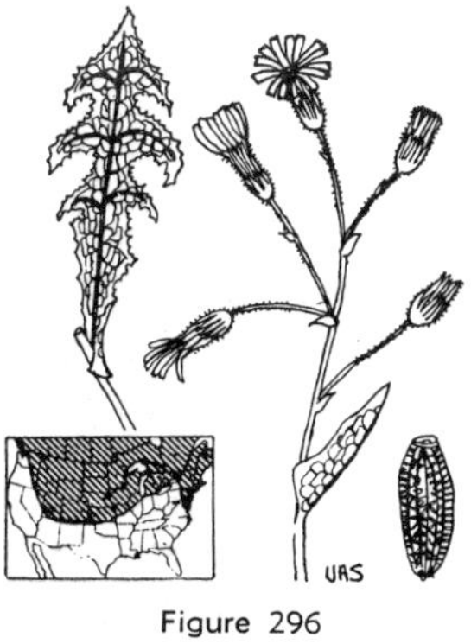

This, in contrast to our other sow-thistles, is a perennial and spreads by an underground system of rootstalks and may thus become a persistent weed. It is a native of Europe and Asia. It has a height of 2 to 4 feet. The lower leaves, sometimes nearly a foot long, have short petioles but the upper ones are clasping. The beautiful bright yellow heads are 1 to 2 inches broad and borne abundantly.

Figure 296

6b Heads about ½ inch high, pale yellow; involucre glabrous or nearly so. 7

7a Leaf-auricles rounded (a); achenes longitudinally ribbed (b).
Fig. 297.   SPINY-LEAVED SOW THISTLE *Sonchus asper* (L.)

This is a European annual that grows up to 5 feet or more. The rather numerous heads are pale yellow; they are about an inch across. The leaves have spines along their edges but are not divided and lobed as in the following species. The lower leaves are spatulate while those of the upper stem are clasping with characteristically rounded auricles. The achenes lack the cross wrinkles between the ridges as possessed by *oleraceus*.

Figure 297

7b Leaf-auricles acute (a); achenes wrinkled crosswise. Fig. 298.
COMMON SOW THISTLE *Sonchus oleraceus* L.

This, another European annual, grows to a height of 1 to 8 feet or more. The lower leaves are definitely petioled and are often deeply cut and lobed and may be nearly a foot long. The upper leaves are clasping with long, sharp-pointed auricles as pictured. All of the members of this genus have milky sap.

Figure 298

**8a Achene with a short stout beak (a); pappus brown; flowers blue to white. Fig. 299.   TALL BLUE LETTUCE *Lactuca biennis integrifolia*
(T. & G.)**

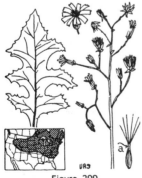

This sparingly-branched plant grows in rather moist soil to a height of 3 to 12 feet. The leaves, up to a foot in length, are tooth-margined and deeply lobed. The pappus is tawny; the achenes have a short neck and the small heads usually light blue are occasionally cream-color.

The genus name refers to the milky sap which is characteristic of all this genus.

Figure 299

8b Achene with a long narrow beak (Fig. 300); pappus white; flowers mainly yellow but sometimes turning bluish. 9

Figure 300

9a Leaf-blades spiny-toothed and often spiny on midrib beneath; head 6 to 12-flowered. Fig. 301.   PRICKLY LETTUCE *Lactuca scariola* L.

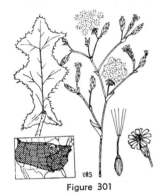

Figure 301

This is a common and widely scattered European weed growing to a height of 2 to 6 feet. The leaves are spiny margined and may be up to 10 inches long. The heads have 8 to 12 pale yellow flowers and are about 1/3 inch across.

GARDEN LETTUCE L. *sativa* L., so well-known, is a closely related plant. There are many varieties of the one species,— Head Lettuce, Curled Lettuce, Asparagus Lettuce, Romaine Lettuce, etc.

9b Leaf-blades without spines on the margins or midribs; heads 12 to 20-flowered. 10

10a Plant smooth throughout. Fig. 302.
                                   WILD LETTUCE *Lactuca canadensis* L.

Figure 302

This is one of our native lettuces; it grows to a height of 3 to 8 feet or more. The leaves are 2 to 8 inches long, the lower ones being deeply lobed while the upper ones are often entire. The many yellow heads measure about ¼ inch across. The pappus is white.

10b Plant more or less hirsute, at least the leaves, with midrib hairy beneath. Fig. 303. HAIRY WOOD-LETTUCE *Lactuca hirsuta* Muhl.

Figure 303

This little native plant grows in dry soil and becomes 1 to 5 feet high. The leaves are 3 to 7 inches long and are pubescent on both sides. The heads are many and about ¼ inch across; the rays are reddish-yellow. The pappus is white.

About 100 species of this genus are known for the Northern Hemisphere.

11a Leaves mostly linear (about 1/6 inch wide); stem rigid, much-branched, striate (with fine lengthwise lines); flowers pink or rose. 12

11b Leaves mostly lanceolate to ovate (¼ inch or more in width); stem not especially rigid, not striate; flowers yellow or whitish (*Prenanthes racemosa* has purplish flowers and striate stem)....13

12a Heads usually 5-flowered, solitary at the end of the branches. Fig. 304. RUSH-LIKE LYGODESMIA *Lygodesmia juncea* (Pursh)

Figure 304

This interesting little dry-ground perennial looks like it might belong to some family other than the Compositae. It is much-branched and spreading with a height of a foot or more. The leaves are linear and up to 2 inches long. The heads are borne at the end of the branches, are a good half-inch across and usually have 5 pink rays.

116

12b Heads usually 8 to 9-flowered, racemose along the branches.
Fig. 305.   BEAKED LYGODESMIA *Lygodesmia rostrata* Gray

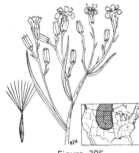

Figure 305

This is a 1 to 3 foot annual growing in the open plains country; the leaves are 2 to 7 inches long and narrow. The heads are about ½ inch across and contain 3 to 10 rose-colored rays; the pappus is white. Another name for these two plants is Prairie Pink. They have often been misplaced in the Pink family by hasty observers.

13a Flowers yellow; heads ½ to one inch broad, mostly erect (some drooping in *Hieracium paniculatum*). 14

13b Flowers greenish, yellowish-white, or purplish; heads ¼ inch broad or less, mostly drooping (erect or spreading in *Prenanthes racemosa*). 17

14a Heads one inch or more broad; leaves coarsely-toothed, acute.
Fig. 306.   CANADA HAWKWEED *Hieracium canadense* Michx.

Figure 306

This dry-woods plant has a height of 1 to 5 feet; it is well supplied with 1 to 3 inch leaves. The orange-yellow heads are about an inch across and, of course, have only rayflowers. The achenes are square cut at the end; the rather heavy pappus is brown.

14b Heads 2/3 inch or less in width; leaves entire, finely-toothed or remotely toothed, obtuse or acute. 15

15a Heads 40 to 50-flowered; peduncles stout, densely-glandular; stem stout; entire plant rough-hairy. Fig. 307.
ROUGH HAWKWEED *Hieracium scabrum* Michx.

Figure 307

This sturdy plant grows to a height of 1 to 3 feet; it is thickly covered with hairs many of which are sometimes glandular. The oblong or sometimes spatulate leaves measure 2 to 4 inches in length and up to 2 inches in width. The yellow heads are smaller than in the preceding species. There is usually but one series of bracts in the rather small involucre; it grows in dry soil.

15b Heads 10 to 20-flowered; peduncles slender, glabrous or somewhat glandular; stem slender. 16

16a Achene fusiform (swollen in middle and tapering to both ends) (a); leaves hairy, obtuse; heads erect. Fig. 308.
HAIRY HAWKWEED *Hieracium gronovii* L.

Figure 308

This is a similar but more slender plant than *scabrum* but of about the same height. The leaves are 2 to 6 inches long, covered with rather dense hair and often definitely petioled. It has many flowering heads measuring ½ inch or a bit more across; the rays are yellow. The achenes are spindle shaped; the pappus is brown. It, too, is found in dry soil.

118

16b Achene columnar (a); leaves glabrous, acute or acuminate; heads often drooping. Fig. 309.

PANICLED HAWKWEED *Hieracium paniculatum* L.

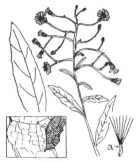

Figure 309

This usually glabrous perennial grows to a height of 1 to 3 feet and belongs to the dry woods. Many of the leaves have petioles and are weakly toothed; they measure up to an inch in width and 6 inches long. The terminal panicle bears a dozen or more yellow heads about ½ inch across. The pappus is rather thin and is brown.

17a Flowers purplish; heads mostly erect or spreading; bracts of the involucre hirsute-pubescent (a). Fig. 310.

GLAUCOUS WHITE LETTUCE *Prenanthes racemosa* Michx.

Figure 310

This and other members of this genus are perennials and are known as Rattle-snake-roots. This species is a sturdy, usually glaucous plant attaining a height of 2 to 6 feet. The leaves are fairly thick, the upper ones sessile and the lower ones 4 to 8 inches long with rather long, margined petioles. The purplish flowers are borne 12 to 15 to each of the many heads, which have a length of about ½ inch.

17b Flowers white, greenish, or yellowish-white; heads drooping; bracts of the involucre glabrous or with a few scattered hairs. 18

119

18a Principal involucre bracts about 5; heads 5 to 7-flowered. Fig. 311.
TALL WHITE LETTUCE *Prenanthes altissima* L.

This woods plant, usually glabrous, grows up to 7 feet high; the stem frequently is tinted with purple. The leaves are thin, and highly variable. The lower ones are often coarsely lobed and have long petioles. The heads are about ½ inch long and have 8 to 15 greenish-yellow flowers surrounded by an involucre of 6 to 10 purplish bracts.

Figure 311

18b Principal involucre bracts 6 to 8; heads 8 to 16-flowered. 19

19a Pappus deep reddish-brown. Fig. 312.
RATTLESNAKE ROOT *Prenanthes alba* L.

This is also called White Lettuce but it has purple stems, greenish-yellow flowers and brown pappus. And it is called Lion's-foot; that's on account of the broad basal leaves which someone thought were about like a lion's track. The suspended heads contain around a dozen flowers and are a little more than ½ inch long. Look for it in the woods.

Figure 312

19b Pappus light brown. Fig. 313.
GALL-OF-THE-EARTH *Prenanthes trifoliolata* (Cass.)

This is a tall plant, arising up to 8 feet or more, but its basal leaves are most distinctive as they are usually three-parted and have long petioles. The 8 to 10 flowers in the drooping heads are whitish and about ½ inch long.

LOW RATTLESNAKE-ROOT *P. trifoliolata nana* (Bigel.) also has trifoliate basal leaves, but this little variety (about 1 foot high) is restricted to the tops of our north-eastern mountains and on north to Labrador.

Figure 313

20a No ray-flowers; all of the flowers of the head with tubular corollas (disk-flowers) only (corolla wanting or reduced in *Ambrosia, Xanthium;* rays sometimes present, if so, usually inconspicuous in *Polymnia, Bidens connata, Tanacetum).* Fig. 314. 21

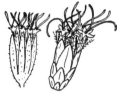

Figure 314

It will be noted that members of the great family Compositae fall into three natural groups. Some species produce flowering heads which contain only ray-flowers (with strap-shaped corollas) of which the Dandelion is a good example. That group has been treated in the preceding pages (Figs. 289 to 313). Now we come to a series of composits in which all of the flowers in each head are tubular. These plants have no ray-flowers. The plants represented by Figures 318 to 381 are of that kind.

20b Both tube-flowers (disk-flower) and ray-flowers present *(Grindelia* and several species of *Bidens* are occasionally rayless). Fig. 315. 67

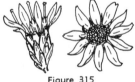

Figure 315

Most common among the composits are the plants which produce a group of tubular-flowers at the center of the head with a ring of showy ray-flowers surrounding them. Plants of this kind begin with Figure 382 and fill the remainder of the book. It may be observed that these ray-flowers have evolved from tubular flowers that grew long and split down one side. Remnants of the 5 lobes of the corolla often remain as tiny teeth at the end of the ray. Since the chief function of these ray-flowers is to make the head conspicuous to attract insect pollinators, they are frequently imperfect and often sterile.

21a Leaves (at least the lower ones) mainly opposite or whorled (in *Polymnia*, the lower leaves are usually alternate, the upper opposite). Fig. 316. .22

Figure 316

21b Leaves alternate (mainly basal in *Elephantopus nudatus.)* Fig. 317. 36

Figure 317

22a Plant a vine. Fig. 318.

CLIMBING BONESET *Mikania scandens* (L.)

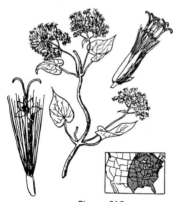

Figure 318

Climbing composits are unusual but that is exactly what we have here. This 5 to 15 foot-long vine lives by scrambling over its up-standing associates. The leaves are heart-shaped with a wavy margin or sometimes weakly toothed and are 2 to 4 inches long. The heads have 4 white or pink flowers and are about ½ inch long. It is found in moist soil, especially in swamps.

22b Plant. erect, not a vine. **23**

23a Heads very small, numerous, in long narrow racemes; staminate and pistillate flowers in separate heads; coarse weedy plant. Fig. 319. GREAT RAGWEED *Ambrosia trifida* L.

Figure 319

This is an almost tree-sized weed with a possible height of nearly 20 feet. It prefers rich moist soil and is quick to take over where good land is neglected. Some of the leaves are undivided but many of them are 3 to 5 lobed and sometimes nearly a foot long. It produces great quantities of pollen and is accused of causing hay fever. Another name is Horse-weed.

23b Heads medium to large, mostly in flat-topped clusters; flowers of the head all perfect (with both stamens and pistils in the same flower) and alike. *(Polymnia* occasionally has inconspicuous rays).** **24**

24a Pappus none (a); flowers yellowish-green or whitish; plant sticky-pubescent. Fig. 320.

SMALL-FLOWERED LEAF-CUP *Polymnia canadensis* L.

This species is keyed here since it sometimes has no ray flowers. For picture and description of the plant turn to Fig. 412.

Figure 320

24b Pappus present; flowers orange, white, pink, lilac, red, purple; plant glabrous or hairy, not viscid (*Eupatorium rugosum* occasionally sticky-pubescent). 25

25a Pappus 2 to 6 rigid awns (a); flowers usually deep yellow or orange. Fig. 321.
SPANISH NEEDLES ....Genus *Bidens* .. page 178

Figure 321

25b Pappus of many fine bristles; flowers white, pink, lilac, red, or purple; heads about ¼ inch broad or less. 26

THOROUGHWORTS Genus Eupatorium

26a Receptacle conic (a); flowers blue or violet. Fig. 322.

MIST FLOWER *Eupatorium coelestinum* L.

Another name for this plant which grows to a height of 1 to 3 feet, usually in moist soil is Blue Boneset. The leaves are petioled, up to 3 inches in length and half that wide; the heads are about ¼ inch high and contain numerous blue or violet flowers.

North America has some 35 thoroughworts but the tropics, where these plants thrive best and other regions bring the world's total up to about 500.

Figure 322

26b Receptacle flat (Fig. 323); flowers mostly white (*Eupatorium purpureum* and *Eupatorium incarnatum* pink to purple). 27

Figure 323

27a Leaf-blades connate-perfoliate. Fig. 324.

COMMON THOROUGHWORT *Eupatorium perfoliatum* L.

Figure 324

This sturdy pubescent plant prefers wet places where it grows up to 5 feet. The long slender leaves are mostly united at their base to surround the stem. The leaves are 4 to 8 inches long and the flowering heads ½ inch or more high. The flowers are almost always white. Boneset is another familiar name for it. It is the only one of our species that has perfoliate leaves.

27b Leaf-blades petioled (a) or sessile (b). Fig. 325. 28

Figure 325

28a Bracts of the involucre mostly equal and in one row (a). Fig. 326. 29

Figure 326

28b Bracts of the involucre in 2 or more rows (a), the outer ones shorter. Fig. 327. 31

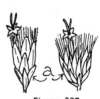

Figure 327

124

29a Flowers pink to purple; leaves deltoid-ovate, usually somewhat hastate. Fig. 328.

PINK THOROUGHWORT *Eupatorium incarnatum* Walt.

Figure 328

This rather frail, sometimes decumbent plant grows in protected areas in sandy soil and has a length of 2 to 4 feet. It is minutely pubescent; the leaves may be 2 inches or more long, are often cordate at the base and have long petioles. The small heads contain some 20 pink or lavender flowers.

29b Flowers white; leaves ovate to ovate-lanceolate. 30

30a Leaves thin, long-petioled (½ to 2½ inches long), sharp-pointed. Fig. 329.   WHITE SNAKEROOT *Eupatorium rugosum* Houtt.

Figure 329

This thin-leaved perennial grows in rich woods to a height of 1 to 4 feet. The heavily serrate leaves are variable in form and measure 3 to 5 inches. The numerous small heads containing 10 to 30 brilliant white flowers are borne in compound corymbs. This plant is poisonous to cattle and even to humans who consume the milk from cows feeding on the plant.

30b Leaves thickish, sessile or short-petioled (2/3 inch or less in length), usually obtuse. Fig. 330.

SMALLER WHITE SNAKEROOT *Eupatorium aromaticum* L.

Figure 330

This plant is smaller (1 to 2 feet) than the preceding species which it resembles and has smaller but stiffer leaves. The leaves have rounded or cordate base and may measure up to 3 inches, with petioles about ½ inch long. The 10 to 25 white flowers are borne in numerous small heads. It grows in dry soil.

31a Leaves whorled in groups of 3 to 6 (a); flowers pink to purple. Fig. 331.   JOE-PYE WEED *Eupatorium purpureum* L.

Figure 331

This sturdy species grows to a height of 3 to 10 feet. It prefers moist soil; it is frequently known as Purple Boneset, on account of the purple or pinkish flowers. The stems are often purple; the leaves are borne in whorls of 3 to 6, are thin and measure from 3 to 12 inches in length. The bracts of the involucre are overlapping in 4 or 5 series.

31b Leaves opposite (upper ones sometimes alternate in *Eupatorium serotinum*); flowers white. 32

32a Leaves linear (less than ¼ inch wide), usually entire, clustered. Fig. 332.

HYSSOP-LEAVED THOROUGHWORT *Eupatorium hyssopifolium* L.

This short rough-puberelent plant seldom exceeds 2 feet in height. The leaves, 2 inches and less in length are linear and very narrow. The crowded cormyb bears numerous heads about 1/3 inch long with bell-shaped involucre and but 4 to 6 white flowers.

E. lecheaefolium Greene, about the same size with a bit smaller flowers and slightly longer leaves is our only other linear-leaved species. It grows on the coastal plains of our South-east.

Figure 332

32b Leaves lanceolate to ovate (½ to 2 inches wide), toothed. 33

33a Leaves long-petioled, the upper ones alternate; heads 10 to 15-flowered. Fig. 333.

LATE FLOWERING THOROUGHWORT *Eupatorium serotinum* Michx.

This plant grows in woods and wet places to a height of 3 to 7 feet. The coarsely-serrated lanceolate to ovate-lanceolate leaves range from 2 to 10 inches in length and are finely pubescent. The flowers are white and the bracts of the involucre have white margins. The achenes are less than 1/10 inch long.

Figure 333

33b Leaves sessile or nearly so; heads mostly 5-flowered. 34

34a Inner involucre bracts ⅜ inch long with white, papery, abruptly-pointed tips; stem one to 3 feet high, harshly-pubescent. Fig. 334.
WHITE THOROUGHWORT *Eupatorium album* L.

Figure 334

This harshly-pubescent species grows in dry areas to a height of 1 to 3 feet. The leaves are prominently veined, coarsely toothed, oblong-lanceolate and 1 to 4 inches long. The bracts of the involucre are longer than the white flowers; the achenes are about ⅛ inch in length.

34b Inner involucre bracts about ¼ inch long; stems 2 to 8 feet high..35

35a Stem densely fine-pubescent; inner involucre bracts with obtuse tips; leaves lanceolate, some with short petioles. Fig. 335.
TALL THOROUGHWORT *Eupatorium altissimum* L.

Figure 335

This downy, heavy-stemmed species grows in dry areas and has a height of 3 to 7 feet. The 1½ to 5 inch leaves are on the linear-lanceolate order with sharp-serrate margins. The flowers are white, about 1/6 inch long; the bracts have pale margins and are a bit longer than the flowers; they are blunt ended.

35b Stem fine-pubescent; inner involucre bracts abruptly short-pointed; leaves ovate to lanceolate, mostly sessile. Fig. 336.
VERVAIN THOROUGHWORT *Eupatorium pilosum* **Walt.**

Figure 336

Such species names as this are rather common and are easily remembered if one knows the plant used as comparison. What is said here is that this is the thoroughwort which has leaves like a verbena. Species names usually tell something about the plant; it helps if one understands it all.

This roughly-pubescent plant stands 3 to 8 feet high and has heads about ¼ inch high which contain 5 white flowers. The leaves are 2 to 4 inches long.

36a Leaves spiny (a); pappus plumose (b).
Fig. 337. (THISTLES) **37**

Figure 337

36b Leaves not spiny (*Xanthium spinosum* with an inch-long spine in each leaf-axil); pappus none or if present not plumose (except in *Liatris, Kuhnia,* and minutely so in *Vernonia*). **41**

37a All the bracts of the involucre with spiny tips; heads deep brilliant violet. Fig. 338. **COMMON THISTLE** *Cirsium vulgare* **(Savi)**

Figure 338

Thistles have a way of protecting themselves; in pastured places the grazing animals keep the other plants eaten down around the thistles and are thus said to "cultivate them", with the result that they grow more luxuriantly than they could otherwise.

This widely-distributed biennial stands 3 to 5 feet high with leaves, as pictured, 3 to 6 inches long. The heads measure 1½ to 2 inches in both length and breadth and are usually solitary at the end of branches. The flowers are dark purple.

37b Some or all of the involucre bracts without spiny tips; heads mostly light purple. 38

38a Leaves at maturity densely white-woolly beneath. 39

38b Leaves at maturity essentially green on both sides (often with a few white hairs beneath). 40

39a Leaves merely toothed, not deeply lobed; outer involucre bracts with tips about ½ as long as the body (a). Fig. 339.

TALL THISTLE *Cirsium altissimum* (L.)

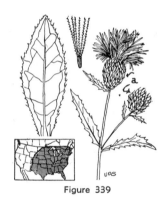

Figure 339

This one grows up to 10 feet high. The leaves are ovate-oblong and frequently clasp the stem; they have a heavy white pubescence on the under side but are only sparingly pubescent above. The serrations of the leaf-margins are prickle pointed. The lower leaves frequently narrow into margined petioles and may be 8 inches long. The light-purple flowers are borne in heads about 2 inches broad.

IOWA THISTLE *C. iowense* Pammel, has larger heads and involucral bracts with longer tips.

39b Leaves deeply lobed or cut; outer involucre bracts with tips about as long as the body (a). Fig. 340.

FIELD THISTLE *Cirsium discolor* (Muhl.)

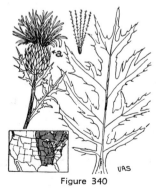

Figure 340

This thistle grows 4 to 6 feet and has rather deeply cut spiny-margined leaves some of which are a foot long, and 2 inches or more in width. The heads are about 1½ inches high and a bit broader. The flowers are pink or light purple and occasionally white. It grows along roadsides and in fields.

40a Outer involucre bracts with spiny tips, inner bracts without spiny tips; heads 2 to 3 inches broad; plant one to 3 feet high. Fig. 341.

PASTURE THISTLE *Cirsium pumilum* (Nutt.)

Figure 341

This rather villous-pubescent plant may attain a height of 2 to 3 feet. Its fragrant flowers are purple or sometimes white and are borne in large terminal heads which often measure 2 to 3 inches across. Many bees are attracted to it both for nectar and pollen. The leaves are 4 to 7 inches long and up to 2 inches in width.

40b None of the involucre bracts spiny-tipped; heads about 1½ inches broad; plant 3 to 8 feet high. Fig. 342.

SWAMP THISTLE *Cirsium muticum* Michx.

Figure 342

This thistle differs from many of the others in searching out moist spots and swamps in which to grow. Its woolly youthful stem becomes nearly bald with maturity when it attains a height of 4 to 8 feet. The leaves (4 to 8 inches long) are often deeply lobed; the purple flowers are borne in heads which measure about 1½ inches across.

Our region has many other species of thistles but most of them belong more definitely to Summer than to Fall.

41a (a, b, c) Flowers yellow or greenish. **42**

41b Flowers white or cream-color *(Cacalia* sometimes pinkish). **48**

41c Flowers purplish, blue, red, pink. **54**

42a Staminate and pistillate flowers in separate heads on same plant; fruit nut-like or a bur, ⅛ to one inch long with few to many spines. **43**

42b Stamens and pistils in the same head; fruit less than ⅛ inch long, ribbed or angled, but not spiny. **45**

43a Bracts of staminate involucre united to form a cup (a); fruit nut-like, about 1/5 inch long, with short blunt spines; leaves deeply pinnatifid. Fig. 343.

HAY-FEVER WEED *Ambrosia artemisiifolia* L.

Figure 343

Here again is a symbolic species name, the "wormwood-leaved ragweed". This annual, growing to a height of 1 to 5 feet, is exceedingly common in late summer and fall in pastures and grain fields. Some thrifty farmers have learned to cut and cure it for winter feed for calves and sheep with surprisingly good results. The numerous large seeds make it a nutritious feed. It is a native of America which has invaded Europe "in exchange" for some of their annoying weeds with which we must contend.

43b Bracts of staminate involucre distinct (Fig. 344); fruit a bur, 1/3 to one inch long, with numerous hooked spines; leaves entire, toothed or shallowly lobed..44

Figure 344

44a Leaves lanceolate with a 3-pronged spine (a) in each axil; bur ¼ to ½ inch long. Fig. 345.

SPINY BURWEED *Xanthium spinosum* L.

Figure 345

This is a European weed now widely scattered with us. It grows 1 to 3 feet high with leaves 2 to 5 inches long. The leaves are covered on their under side with a white-canescence and arise out of the axil of a three-pronged spine. As though these diabolical spines were not enough, its fruit is a spine covered bur containing two seeds. The following and several other native species bear similar burs but none has leaves or spines like this species.

132

**44b Leaves broadly ovate, no spines in the axils; bur ½ to one inch
long. Fig. 346.   BEACH CLOTBUR *Xanthium echinatum* Murr.**

Figure 346

The farmer (and who hasn't had experience with them?) seldom stops to enquire just which one of the several Cockleburs infests his ground. Most of them grow 2 to 3 feet high and are at their best in low sandy areas. This species is characterized by the dense prickles and brown pubescence on the burs.

AMERICAN COCKLEBUR *X. chinense* Mill., which is likely the most abundant in many regions, has burs and their prickles practically devoid of any pubescence.

**45a Pappus of numerous white fine bristles; foliage not strong-scented;
stem hollow. Fig. 347.**

COMMON GROUNDSEL *Senecio vulgaris* L.

Figure 347

This European weed which grows to a height of a foot or more is widely scattered. The pinnately divided leaves are 2 to 6 inches long and often clasping at the base. The heads are ¼ inch across and somewhat higher. The involucral bracts are black-tipped; the disk-flowers are yellowish; there are no ray-flowers. The achenes are hair-covered and bear a white pappus.

Several other species of the genus belong to Spring or Summer.

**45b Pappus none or a short crown; foliage strong-scented; stem
solid.** **46**

**46a Heads ¼ to ½ inch broad, in a corymb; pappus a short crown (a).
Fig. 348.** **TANSY** *Tanacetum vulgare* L.

Figure 348

This is an old garden favorite which was once much grown for medicinal purposes and for seasoning. It is of European origin but maintains itself if not too vigorously molested. It is practically glabrous and grows to a height of some 3 feet. The foliage is a deep green and has a characteristic odor. The much-cut leaves are up to a foot in length; the numerous heads are ¼ inch or a bit broader and bear many tiny yellow flowers.

46b Heads 1/6 inch or less broad, in a panicle; pappus none. 47

47a Leaves densely white-hairy beneath; leaf divisions linear to lanceolate. Fig. 349. **COMMON MUGWORT** *Artemisia vulgaris* L.

Figure 349

This glabrous perennial may have a height of 3 feet with leaves 4 inches long; they are covered on the under side with a dense growth of white hairs, but are smooth and dark green above. All of the flowers are tubular but only the central ones are fertile. The heads are less than ¼ inch across. It is of European origin and grows widely in waste places with us.

47b Leaves glabrous or only slightly pubescent; leaf divisions threadlike. Fig. 350. **TALL WORMWOOD** *Artemisia caudata* Michx.

Figure 350

This native biennial may attain a height of 6 feet. It grows best in sandy places. The heads are very small and are borne in great numbers in tall compact pannicles. The leaves are finely divided into many linear lobes.

LINEAR-LEAVED W O R M W O O D *A. glauca dracunculina* (S. Wats.), growing 2 to 4 feet high and having simple linear leaves up to 3 inches long, is another late flowering species. It grows from Illinois westward to the Pacific.

48a Plants resinous-dotted; pappus bristles very plumose (a); anthers not united. Fig. 351.

FALSE BONESET *Kuhnia eupatorioides* L. This plant standing up to 3 feet in height has lanceolate leaves measuring up to 4 inches and having rather shallow scattered teeth. The lower leaves have petioles while those higher on the stem are sessile. The heads, about 1/3 inch high bear several cream-colored flowers. The feathery pappus is tawny to white.

PRAIRIE FALSE BONESET *K. eupatorioides corymbulosa* T. & G., ranging from Illinois westward has larger and more thickly clustered heads and sharply serrate leaves. Both species are found in dry soil.

Figure 351

48b Plants not resinous-dotted; pappus bristles smooth or slightly rough; anthers united. **49**

49a Plants glabrous or hairy (but not densely white-woolly); leaves toothed or cut (Fig. 352). **50**

Figure 352

49b At least some parts of the plant (usually the under side of the leaves) densely white-woolly; leaves entire or wavy-margined (Fig. 353). **51**

Figure 353

50a Plant with milky-juice; leaves lanceolate to ovate-lanceolate; involucre conspicuously swollen at the base before flowering. Fig. 354.   FIRE-WEED *Erechtites hieracifolia* (L.)

This plant may grow as tall as 8 feet though it is often much shorter. It grows in sheltered places; it gets its name from being one of the first plants to re-vegetate burned-over areas. The leaves are thin and 2 to 8 inches long. The heads, ½ inch or more in height bear several whitish flowers with a shining white pappus.

Figure 354

135

50b Plant without milky juice; leaves triangular-lanceolate or hastate; involucre cylindric. Fig. 355.

SWEET-SCENTED INDIAN PLANTAIN *Cacalia suaveolens* L.

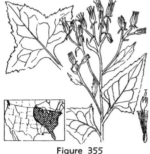

This glabrous plant has a height of 3 to 5 feet. It grows in shaded places and has triangular leaves with irregular serrations and margined petioles. The leaves measure 4 to 9 inches in length. The heads are about ½ inch high and bear 20 to 30 white perfect flowers.

Figure 355

51a Stamens on one plant, pistils on another plant; involucre bracts pearly-white. Fig. 356.

PEARLY EVERLASTING *Anaphalis margaritacea* (L.)

This plant is covered with a rather dense white woolly coat and grows to a possible height of 3 feet. The almost linear leaves are sessile; they measure 3 to 5 inches long and are sometimes nearly smooth and green above but with a tangled white pubescence beneath. The numerous globular heads are about ¼ inch high. It grows in dry soil and often in dry places in the woods.

Figure 356

51b Both stamens and pistils on the same plant; involucre bracts brownish or yellowish-white. 52

52a Plant less than 12 inches high, loosely branched and spreading; heads mainly terminal. Fig. 357.

LOW CUDWEED *Gnaphalium uliginosum* L.

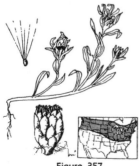

This rather decumbent plant has a stem length of less than a foot and has a white woolly covering. The leaves are an inch or more in length. The small globular heads are surrounded by leafy bracts. It grows in damp soil.

Figure 357

136

52b Plants over 12 inches high, erect, somewhat branched above; heads corymbose or paniculate-corymbose. 53

53a Leaves decurrent (extending down the stem); stem sticky-pubescent. Fig. 358.

CLAMMY EVERLASTING *Gnaphalium macounii* Greene

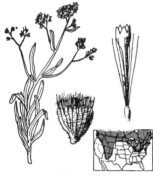

It grows to a height of 2 to 3 feet; the lanceolate leaves are 1 to 3 inches long and covered on the under side with a dense white woolly pubescence. The heads are about ¼ inch high. It is also known as Balsam Weed.

Figure 358

53b Leaves sessile, not decurrent; plant pubescent, but not sticky. Fig. 359. SWEET BALSAM *Gnaphalium obtusifolium praecox* Fern.

This rather common plant of dry places grows to a height of 1 to 3 feet. It, too, is covered with a tangled white woolly pubescence. The leaves are 1 to 3 inches long. The slender heads are about ¼ inch high. The bracts of the involucre are white, sometimes with a brown tinge. The achenes are glabrous.

Figure 359

54a Receptacle densely bristly; bracts deeply fringed or with slender hooked tips. Fig. 360. 55

Figure 360

54b Receptacle naked; bracts neither deeply fringed nor with hooked tips. 56

**55a Bracts deeply fringed (a); leaves mostly lanceolate, narrowed at
the base. Fig. 361.   BLACK KNAPWEED *Centaurea nigra* L.**

Figure 361

This is a weed which is native of Europe; it grows to a height of 1 to 2 feet and is found in waste places. Like all weeds, too much attention should not be given to its reported distribution, for such plants are introduced in many ways and are likely to pop up almost any place. It has a height of 2 feet and is roughly pubescent. The leaves are 3 to 6 inches long and the flowers purplish-red.

**55b Bracts with hooked tips (a); leaves ovate, usually cordate at the
base. Fig. 362.   COMMON BURDOCK *Arctium minus* Bernh.**

Figure 362

This later blooming and smaller burdock is limited to about 5 feet in height; its big cousin, *A. lappa* L. may grow to twice that height. Both have large leaves with wavy margins and often cordate base and sometimes 1½ feet long. The heads, up to 1 inch broad in *lappa* and smaller in *minus* have involucral bracts with an effective hook at the end which hold the entire bur to passing animals for seed distribution. The flowers are purplish, pink or sometimes white and largely hidden by the bracts. These plants often choose rich soil in which to make their luxuriant growth. Both are European.

**56a Pappus bristles plumose (a) or barbellate (b)
(Fig. 363); plants simple or little-branched; heads
in elongate spikes or racemes. 57**

Figure 363

**56b Pappus bristles simple, not plumose nor barbellate
(Fig. 364); plants usually branched; heads in a broad,
rather flat-topped cluster. 61**

Figure 364

138

57a Pappus very plumose (c); heads usually 15 to 60-flowered.
Fig. 365a.   SCALY BLAZING STAR *Liatris squarrosa* **Willd.**

This interesting little prairie plant has a height of 1 to 2 feet and leaves 3 to 5 inches long. The heads are borne in the axils of the leaves, alternating on the somewhat zig-zag stem. The heads are ½ inch or more across and bear 12 to 50 purplish flowers.

CYLINDRIC BLAZING STAR *L. cylindracea* Michx. (363b) differs from the above in having more-rounded, closely appressed bracts. It grows in dry soil from Minnesota and Illinois, westward.

Figure 365

57b Pappus barbellate. Fig. 366. . . . .**58**

Figure 366

58a Involucre bracts with acute spreading tips; heads mostly 3 to 6-flowered; inflorescence very dense. Fig. 367.
PRAIRIE BUTTON-SNAKEROOT *Liatris pycnostachya* **Michx.**

This linear to linear-lanceolate leaved plant has a height of 2 to 5 feet with leaves up to 10 inches long. The heads are ½ inch or less in length, are thickly placed in a spike-like arrangement on the stem and bear 3 to 6 purplish flowers. It is a remnant of our wonderful prairie flora and still may be found growing luxuriantly in favored spots.

Figure 367

58b Involucre bracts mostly with obtuse or rounded appressed (not spreading) tips (Fig. 368); heads 5 to 45-flowered. **59**

Figure 368

59a Heads roundish, 15 to 45-flowered; leaves linear to elliptic, often broadly so; plant pubescent. Fig. 369.

LARGE BUTTON-SNAKEROOT *Liatris scariosa* Willd.

Figure 369

This usually finely-pubescent plant grows in dry soil and attains a height of 2 to 5 feet. The long lower leaves have a margined petiole; the upper ones are shorter and nearly linear. The scattered heads alternate on the stem and may attain a width of an inch; they contain 15 to 45 bluish-purple flowers. It is sometimes known as Blue Blazing-star.

59b Heads oblong, 5 to 13-flowered; leaves linear; plant mostly glabrous. 60

60a Leaves ciliate, at least near base (a); inflorescence generally not dense; pappus reddish-purple. Fig. 370.

LOOSE-FLOWERED BUTTON-SNAKEROOT *Liatris graminifolia*
(Walt.)

Figure 370

This grass-leaved blazing-star grows in dry soil and has a height of 2 to 3 feet. All the leaves are narrow and carry definite punctations. The heads are narrow and bear 5 to 13 reddish-purple flowers. The involucre is frequently resinous.

DOTTED BUTTON-SNAKEROOT *L. punctata* Hook., with leaves and bracts heavily punctate is found in dry soil from Minnesota and Missouri westward. It has broader heads and more rounded bracts, with 4 to 6 flowers per head.

60b Leaves not ciliate; inflorescence usually dense; pappus brownish-yellow. Fig. 371. DENSE BLAZING STAR *Liatris spicata* (L.)

Figure 371

Growing sometimes to a height of 6 feet this plant displays its heads in a dense spike frequently more than a foot long. The heads are ¼ inch or more in width and have 5 to 12 bluish-purple flowers (rarely white). The leaves are linear, the upper ones very narrow. It grows in moist soil.

61a Heads 2 to 5-flowered; pappus composed of several rigid bristles terminating scale-like bases (a). Fig. 372. 62

Figure 372

61b Heads many-flowered; pappus (at least in part) of numerous fine bristles. 63

62a Leaves mainly on the stem and branches. Fig. 373.
CAROLINA ELEPHANT'S-FOOT *Elephantopus carolinianus* Willd.

Figure 373

This is a dry soil plant growing to a height of 2 to 3 feet. The leaves are thin, oval and measure up to 8 inches in length. Several narrow heads, each with 2 to 5 purplish flowers, are gathered together at the end of the stem and surrounded by broad bracts, as pictured. Apparently the broad lower leaves account for the "elephant-foot" name.

62b Leaves mainly basal; stem naked or with a few bract-like leaves. Fig. 374.

SMOOTHISH ELEPHANT'S-FOOT *Elephantopus nudatus* Gray

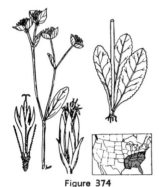

This is a smaller plant with narrower leaves than the above with fewer leaves on the stems. The lower leaves are spatulate shaped and thin and green.

WOOLLY ELEPHANT'S-FOOT *E. tomentosus* L., a villous-pubescent plant of similar size but with broader basal leaves grows through the South from Virginia to Arkansas and southward. The flowers and heads are much the same in all three of these species.

Figure 374

63a Pappus single, of fine bristles; leaves one to 3 inches wide; plant camphor-scented, found mostly in salt marshes. Fig. 375.

SALT-MARSH FLEABANE *Pluchea camphorata* (L.)

This nearly glabrous, 3-foot plant bears leaves as pictured, up to 8 inches in length. The heads are about ¼ inch high and bear many tiny purplish flowers. Found in fresh or brackish marshes. It is also called Stinkweed. Plants of this genus in our area have purplish to pink flowers and emit a strong camphor-like odor.

Figure 375

63b Pappus double, the inner (a) of fine bristles, the outer (b) of much shorter scale-like bristles (Fig. 376); leaves 1½ inches wide or less; plants not camphor-scented, found in thickets, prairies, and open places but not in salt marshes. 64

Figure 376

64a Most of the involucre bracts with slender tips 2 or 3 times their own length (a); mostly 30 to 40 flowers in a head. Fig. 377.

NEW YORK IRONWEED *Vernonia noveboracensis* Willd.

This usually rough-pubescent plant grows in moist places in pastures and elsewhere and may have a height of 8 feet. The lanceolate leaves are 4 to 10 inches long and up to an inch in width. The heads, nearly ½ inch across, produce around 30 deep purple flowers with brownish-purple to greenish bracts and purplish pappus.

Figure 377

64b Involucre bracts (a) obtuse or acute, not filiform-tipped. Fig. 378. 65

Figure 378

65a Leaves densely-hairy beneath; heads mostly 35 to 50-flowered. Fig. 379. PRAIRIE IRONWEED *Vernonia missurica* Raf.

This is a tomentose prairie plant of 3 to 5 feet; it has lanceolate leaves 5 inches in length and an inch or more wide. The heads bear purplish bracts, are about ½ inch broad and contain 35 to 50 small deep-purple flowers. The pappus is purplish or tawny.

This genus has some 10 or more species in our region. Over 500 species have been named, world wide, a large percentage of which are in South America where the genus is at its best.

Figure 379

65b Leaves glabrous or only slightly pubescent beneath; heads mostly 20 to 30-flowered. 66

66a Heads in a loose cluster; plant 4 to 10 feet high; leaves mostly lanceolate, 4 to 12 inches long. Fig. 380.

TALL IRONWEED *Vernonia altissima* **Nutt.**

Figure 380

This smooth, lanceolate-leaved plant is truly "tall" being sometimes 10 feet high with leaves up to a foot in length. The heads are about ¼ inch broad and have 10 to 25 reddish-purple flowers. The bracts are appressed and the pappus purple. It is a prairie plant, preferring moist soil.

66b Heads in a dense cluster; plant 2 to 6 feet high; leaves lanceolate to linear-lanceolate, 3 to 6 inches long. Fig. 381.

WESTERN IRONWEED *Vernonia fasciculata* **Michx.**

Figure 381

This usually-smooth plant has a height of 2 to 5 feet with lanceolate leaves up to 6 inches in length. The heads have around 25 reddish-purple flowers and measure about ¼ inch across. It is a prairie plant preferring rich soil. The achenes are usually glabrous and the pappus purple.

67a Pappus of disk-flowers of 2 or 3 stiff awns (a); heads very resinous; all flowers yellow. Fig. 382.

BROAD-LEAVED GUM-PLANT *Grindelia squarrosa* (Pursh)

Figure 382

A dry-soil glabrous branching plant growing to a height of 1 to 2 feet. Lower leaves oblong-spatulate; upper ones as pictured, often clasping. Bracts of involucre with tips recurving (squarose) and covered with sticky gum.

NARROW-LEAVED GUM-PLANT *G. lanceolata* Nutt., with linear leaves and the bracts not squarose is a dry-land plant of similar height growing from Kansas to Tennessee and southward.

67b Not as in 67a. **68**

68a Pappus a circle of thin chaff-like scales. (Fig. 383a). **69**

68b Not as in 68a. **70**

69a The 4 to 5 broad ray-flowers, white. Fig. 383.

GALINSOGA *Galinsoga ciliata* Blake

This weak-stemmed pubescent plant grows to a height of 1 to 2 feet or more and is a most persistent weed. The disk-flowers are yellow, and their achenes are tipped with aristate pappus.

G. parviflora Cav., a highly similar species, is less common. The pappus of the disk achenes have no awns.

Still another introduced species, *G. caracasana* (DC.), has purple ray-flowers instead of white.

Figure 383

69b The 10 or more ray-flowers yellow; disk globular, yellow.
Fig. 384. YELLOW SNEEZEWEED *Helenium autumnale* L.

Figure 384

This sturdy plant is abundant in wet pastures and swamps. It grows 2 to 6 feet high. The heads are 1 to 2 inches broad with 10 to 20 drooping yellow rays and numerous yellow disk-flowers (also yellow).

PURPLE-HEAD SNEEZEWEED *H. nudiflorum* Nutt., a somewhat smaller plant with similar leaves and with yellow, often brown marked, rays and purplish disk ranges from Missouri to North Carolina and southward, while FINE-LEAVED SNEEZEWEED *H. tenuifolium* Nutt. has filiform leaves, yellow heads and grows from Kansas to Virginia and southward.

70a Pappus, at least of the disk-flowers, of slender hair-like bristles (a); ray-flowers, pistillate (without anthers or pollen). Fig. 385. ....**71**

Figure 385

70b Pappus none (a) or sometimes represented by a crown (b), a few awns (c), or chaff-like scales or minute bristles. Fig. 386. ....**81**

Figure 386

71a Ray-flowers not yellow. **72**

71b Ray-flowers yellow. **76**

72a Corolla of both the disk-flowers and the ray-flowers white; white-hirsuit-pubescent plant. (See Fig. 453).
WHITE GOLDEN-ROD *Solidago bicolor* L.

This is our one white golden-rod (sometimes pale yellow). Turn to page 170.

72b Corolla of the disk-flowers yellow (often turning red, brown or purplish in the asters.) **73**

Figure 387

73a Scales of involucre (a) in several rows and length, overlapping. Fig. 387. ASTERS ....Genus *Aster* .... page 157

73b Scales of involucre (a) in but 1 or 2 rows, narrow and scarcely overlapping. Fig. 388. 74

Figure 388

74a Heads very small and numerous, rays inconspicuous, scarcely longer than the pappus. Fig. 389.

HORSE-WEED *Erigeron canadensis* L.

Figure 389

This hairy plant (sometimes smooth) growing to a height of 1 to 8 feet, is a very common weed and is now scattered almost world-wide. The leaves (1 to 4 inches) are linear, sparingly toothed and very abundant. In the earlier stages the stem is unbranched and the many erect leaves makes the name "Colt's-tail" seem very appropriate. The tiny white rays are particularly numerous in the many small heads (⅛ inch high of less).

LOW HORSE-WEED *Erigeron divaricatus* Michx., is a much branching little plant which grows only 3 to 12 inches high. The rays are purplish; the hairy leaves entire and seldom over an inch long. It ranges through the central United States.

74b Rays long and slender, white or purplish tinted. 75

75a Stem leaves mostly with sharp teeth; stem with spreading hairs. Fig. 390.

WHITE-TOP *Erigeron annuus* (L.)

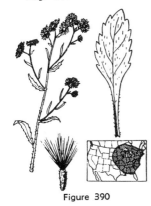

Figure 390

The members of this genus are natives of our country but are now widely disseminated as weeds. This species (1 to 4 feet) is very common in meadows and fields. The heads are around ½ inch broad and have 40 to 70 rays, usually white but frequently purple tinted. At least the disk flowers have a circle of short bristles or scales below and outside the longer slender hairs, making the pappus "double".

147

75b Stem leaves linear, mostly without teeth on margins; stem with appressed hairs. Fig. 391.

DAISY-FLEABANE *Erigeron strigosus* Muhl.

Figure 391

This species is similar to the preceding, with which it grows, but is somewhat smaller. Both are annuals. The lower leaves are spatulate with long, slender petioles.

There are several other species of this genus in our area but they belong more particularly to Summer and to Spring.

76a Pappus double (in the disk flowers at least), (with a whorl of long hairs above or inside another whorl of shorter ones). (See Fig. 392b). 77

76b Pappus simple (with but one whorl of equal parts). (See Fig. 397a). 80

77a Achenes of ray-flowers thick, with only a circular crown at top (a); achenes of disk-flowers flattened, with double pappus (b). Fig. 392. HETEROTHECA *Heterotheca subaxillaris* (Lam.)

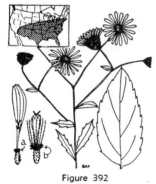

Figure 392

This annual or biennal grows in dry soil to a height of 1 to 3 feet. The upper leaves are clasping while the lower ones, measuring some 3 inches, have slender petioles. The yellow heads are ½ inch or more across and have 15 to 25 slender rays. The disk flowers have two circles of pappus, the outer one quite short, but the ray flowers are devoid of capillary structures.

77b Both ray-flowers and disk-flowers with flattened achenes and double pappus. 78

78a Leaves grass-like, linear; plant covered with silvery pubescence. Fig. 393.
GRASS-LEAVED GOLDEN ASTER *Chrysopsis graminifolia* (Michx.)

This plant, white with silvery pubescence, grows up to 3 feet high, in dry soil. The soft grass-like leaves vary from tiny ones on the upper stems to as much as a foot in length at the base of the plant. Both the rays and disk flowers are yellow and make the heads ½ inch broad.

SICKLE-LEAVED GOLDEN ASTER C. *falcata* (Pursh), a low eastern coastal plant otherwise similar, blooms somewhat earlier.

Figure 393

78b Leaves broader; plants not silvery. 79

79a Heads many; pubescence long, but falling away. Fig. 394.
MARYLAND GOLDEN ASTER *Chrysopsis mariana* (L.)

This sturdy 2-foot plant, covered when young with a tangled silky pubescence but becoming glabrous at maturity has oblong or lanceolate leaves 2 to 4 inches long. The stems supporting the inch-broad heads are covered with sticky hair as are also the bracts. It is found in dry soil.

Figure 394

79b Heads fewer; at ends of branches; plants thickly covered with tangled appressed hairs. Fig. 395.
HAIRY GOLDEN ASTER *Chrysopsis bakeri* Greene

In contrast to the foregoing this somewhat similar species is permanently pubescent; the leaves are shorter (1 to 2 inches) and the yellow heads a bit larger, but less abundant.

Other species, *stenophylla*, *pilosa*, and *hispida*, usually smaller but somewhat similar, grow in the western part of our area.

Figure 395

80a Heads **very numerous, small, less than ½ inch across; bracts in several series, overlapping (a).** Fig. 396. **GOLDENRODS** .... page 170

Figure 396

80b Heads few; 2 inches or more across. Fig. 397.
ELECAMPANE *Inula helenium* L.

Figure 397

This sturdy European perennial growing up to 6 feet is now widely scattered over our area. The lower leaves have long petioles and may measure nearly a foot in width by well over that in length. The fairly large upper leaves are sessile. The heads are wholly yellow and 2 to 4 inches across. The achenes are quadrangular and smooth. It is found in fields and roadsides.

81a Receptacle with chaffy scales or bristles between the flowers...82

81b Receptacle not as in 81a, naked; achenes much flattened with winged margins (a). Fig. 398.
ASTER-LIKE BOLTONIA *Boltonia asteroides* (L.)

Figure 398

This sturdy plant with a possible height of 8 feet produces heads an inch or more across with pink, white or purple ray-flowers. The rays are pistillate, while the disk-flowers are perfect. The yellow lanceolate leaves are 2 to 6 inches long. It grows in moist soil.
PANICLED BOLTONIA *B. diffusa* Ell., a dry-soil plant growing from South Carolina to Missouri and southward, with narrow leaves only 1 or 2 inches long, has much smaller heads (rays usually white).

82a Ray-flowers not producing achenes (though sometimes with a pistil) (occasionally no ray-flowers). 83

82b Ray-flowers seed bearing; pistillate. 91

83a Flowers borne on a flattened receptacle, yellow. 84

150

83b Flowers borne on a convex (a) or column-like (b) receptacle. Fig. 399. 85

Figure 399

84a (a, b, c) Achenes with 2 to 6 barbed awns (a) (spines). Fig. 400.   SPANISH NEEDLES Genus *Bidens* page 178

Figure 400

84b Achenes with 2 to 4 deciduous awns (falling away early) not barbed. Fig. 401.
SUNFLOWERS Genus *Helianthus* page 182

Figure 401

84c Achenes with but 2 short teeth (a), not barbed. Fig. 402.
TALL TICKSEED *Coreopsis tripteris* L.

Figure 402

This smooth perennial with height up to 8 feet has its lower leaves compound or 3-divided and the upper ones lanceolate, all with entire margins. The 6 to 10 broad yellow rays are without notches at the tip and the heads an inch or more in width. It grows in woods and damp places.

Several other species are common, but they bloom earlier and would belong to a summer grouping.

85a Ray-flowers yellow or orange (sometimes ornamented with red or brown). 86

85b Ray flowers white, pink or purplish. 90

86a (a, b, c) Leaves usually alternate; achenes 4 angled; pappus absent or a circle of short teeth. 87

86b Leaves usually opposite; pappus 2 to 4 deciduous awns (a) (usually falling away early), not barbed. (See Fig. 401).
SUNFLOWERS Genus *Helianthus* page 182

86c Leaves alternate above on a winged-stem, the lower ones usually opposite; the pappus 2 to 3 smooth awns (a), not falling away. Fig. 403.   WING-STEM *Actinomeris alternifolia* (L.)

Figure 403

This perennial grows in rich soil to a height of 5 to 9 feet and rather closely resembles the sunflowers. The upper part of the stem is usually winged. The ovate-lanceolate leaves are 4 to 12 inches long and up to 2 or 3 inches wide. The heads are 1 to 2 inches broad and have 2 to 10 irregular yellow rays. The achenes are flattened (or 3-sided if produced by the ray-flowers); the pappus is persistent.

87a Lower leaves 3 to 7 pinnately divided (a), thin; disk elongating in fruit. Fig. 404.

TALL CONE-FLOWER *Rudbeckia laciniata* L.

Figure 404

This glabrous much-branched plant grows in moist ground to a height of 3 to 10 feet, with large leaves sometimes nearly a foot wide. The heads have 6 to 10 bright yellow drooping rays and are 2 to 4 inches across. The disk is greenish-yellow.

GOLDEN-GLOW *R. l. hortensia* Bailey, a very common cultivated ornamental, double (all ray-flowers) is a mutant variety.

88b All of the leaves simple, with scattered serrations or with a smooth margin. Fig. 405.

ORANGE CONE-FLOWER *Rudbeckia fulgida* Ait.

This hair-covered perennial grows 1 to 3 feet high and prefers dry soil. The leaves are 2 to 4 inches long. The few heads are 1 to 1½ inches broad and have 10 to 15 brilliant colored rays; the disks are brown or purplish and about ½ inch across.

BLACK-EYED SUSAN *R. hirta* L., also has simple leaves. It has about the same height, is a somewhat coarser plant with broader heads of 10 to 20 orange rays and is quite hispid. It ranges over much of our territory.

Figure 405

89a Leaves thin; with long hairs; biennial. Fig. 406.

THIN-LEAVED CONE-FLOWER *Rudbeckia triloba* L.

It grows in moist places and is up to 5 feet tall. The upper leaves are lanceolate while the lower ones are usually 3-lobed; all are serrate. Four inches is about the maximum leaf length. The heads are about 2 inches broad and have 8 to 12 ray-flowers. The disk measures about ½ inch across; it is dark purple while the usually yellow rays are sometimes marked at the base with purplish brown or orange. It is sometimes called Brown-eyed Susan, but most any flower with a dark center may be called that.

Figure 406

89b Leaves thick, densely covered with fine pubescence; perennial. pubescence; perennial.

Fig. 407. SWEET CONE-FLOWER *Rudbeckia subtomentosa* Pursh

This is a prairie plant growing up to 6 feet high. The upper leaves are lanceolate but the lower ones are 3 parted and 3 to 5 inches long. The margins are usually serrate. There are 15 to 20 rays to the heads with a brown disk about ½ inch broad and the entire head measuring 2 to 3 inches. The pappus is a short crown topping the achene.

Figure 407

90a Rays white, disk yellow, leaves finely cut and divided, fetid.
 Fig. 408.   MAYWEED *Anthemis cotula* L.

Figure 408

This is a very common weed of barn yards and neglected rich soil. It is an annual with a height of 1 to 2 feet and possesses a strong characteristic odor. The numerous heads are about 1 inch broad with 10 to 20 white rays and with yellow disk-flowers covering a hemispherical receptacle. There is no pappus; the achenes have 10 longitudinal ribs.

90b Rays purple, crimson or pink; leaves simple; disk dark greenish-brown. Fig. 409.

PURPLE CONE-FLOWER *Echinacea purpurea* (L.)

Figure 409

This is a 2 to 5 foot plant growing in moist soils. The stems, often smooth, are sometimes roughened with bristles. The leaves are rather heavily serrate, 3 to 8 inches long. The large showy heads have 16 to 20 long rays giving the heads a width of 3 to 5 inches.

NARROW-LEAVED PURPLE CONE-FLOWER *E. angustifolia* DC., is a dry-soil plant heavily hirsuit 1 to 2 feet high. It has narrow leaves and ranges through the Middle West from Saskatchewan to Texas.

92a Leaves alternate, heads small. Rays white. Fig. 410.

VIRGINIA CROWNBEARD *Verbesina virginica* L.

Figure 410

This is a big plant with little flowers, the heads being scarcely over ½ inch across and the plant 3 to 6 feet high, with leaves up to 10 inches long. There are only 3 to 5 rays to a head; the achenes have 2 slender awns as pictured (sometimes absent). It grows in dry soil.

SMALL YELLOW CROWNBEARD *V. occidentalis* (L.), with 1 to 5 yellow rays in heads up to 1 inch broad, and with opposite leaves is found in dry soil on much of the eastern half of our area. It stands 3 to 7 feet high.

92b Leaves opposite; heads large; rays yellow. Fig. 411.

OX-EYE *Heliopsis helianthoides* (L.)

Figure 411

This glabrous plant has a height of 3 to 5 feet; the leaves are occasionally in whorls of 3 but usually opposite and up to 6 inches long. The heads are around 2 inches broad. There is no pappus, or occasionally there are 2 to 4 teeth on the smooth achenes.

ROUGH OX-EYE *H. helianthoides scabra* (Dunal.) is a similar but rougher plant 2 to 4 feet high. The ovate leaves are 2 to 5 inches long and coarsely serrate. It is widely distributed.

93a Ray-flowers whitish, usually minute or absent. Fig. 412.

SMALL-FLOWERED LEAF-CUP *Polymnia canadensis* L.

Figure 412

This slender 2-to-5-foot plant growing in moist shady places is covered with a sticky pubescence. The leaves are petioled and very thin; the lower ones sometimes as much as 10 inches long, are cut and lobed as pictured. The rather few heads measure from 1/3 to ½ inch across, the bracts often exceeding the rays, though the rays may occasionally be as much as ½ inch long. The short thick achenes have no pappus.

93b Rays yellow, conspicuous; heads large. 94

94a The tall stem practically leafless but with scales; basal leaves
large. Fig. 413.   PRAIRIE DOCK *Silphium terebinthinaceum* Jacq.

Figure 413

This glabrous-stemmed plant of
the prairies and dry woods has a
height of 4 to 10 feet, with substan-
tially all of its leaves basal, and
large (sometimes a foot long and
half that wide) and roughened with
scales. The many heads measure 2
to 3 inches across and have 12 to 20
yellow rays. The achenes bear narrow wings but no pappus except occasionally 2 small teeth. It is also
called Prairie Burdock and Rosin-
plant.

94b Stem with leaves, opposite, alternate or whorled. 95

95a Leaves opposite, not deeply cut. 96

95b Leaves alternate, the lower ones with long petioles and deeply
lobed as pictured. Fig. 414.

COMPASS-PLANT *Silphium laciniatum* L.

Figure 414

This highly-resinous plant grows to a
height of 6 to 10 feet. It belongs to the
prairie but has been too tough to succumb
to man's inroads and persists widely along
road sides and in neglected land. All the
members of the genus have resinous sap
but this one secretes such quantities that
it is known as Rosin-weed, (a name sometimes applied to the whole genus.) The
heads have 15 to 30 pale yellow rays and
measure 2 to 5 inches across. It's only
the ray flowers that produce "seeds" in
this genus.

96a Stem square; upper leaves joined at base to form a "cup".
Fig. 415.   CUP-PLANT *Silphium perfoliatum* L.

This sturdy, usually - glabrous plant grows to a height of 5 to 8 feet. The lower leaves, up to a foot in length and 8 inches wide, have margined petioles. The heads are 2 to 3 inches broad, and bear 18 to 30 light yellow rays. It grows in moist places and is fairly common.

Carl Fritz Henning, a well known park naturalist, once told us — "One of the most beautiful sights I know of is to see a Goldfinch drinking from the cup on a blossoming Cup-Plant."

Figure 415

96b Stem cylindric; upper leaves sessile but not united. Fig. 416.
ENTIRE-LEAVED ROSIN-WOOD *Silphium integrifolium* Michx.

This smaller plant grows 2 to 5 feet in height and varies from glabrous to quite hairy or rough. The leaves may have entire margins or be sometimes rather feebly toothed. The heads expand to 1 to 2 inches broad and have 15 to 25 rays which produce achenes as pictured. The disk-flowers are sterile.

WHORLED ROSIN-WEED S. *trifoliatum* L., growing in woods as far north as Ohio, is characterized by small heads and lanceolate leaves which are in whorls of 3.

Figure 416

ASTERS Genus Aster

**1a At least the basal leaves with both a petiole and a
heart-shaped (cordate) blade. Fig. 417.** 2

Figure 417

**1b None of the leaves both heart-shaped and stalked (some sessile
heart-shaped leaves are common among some of the asters falling
both under 1a and 1b).** 9

2a Ray-flowers colored. 3

2b Ray-flowers white; leaves thin and smooth, at least on upper surface; plants not glandular. Fig. 418.

WHITE WOOD ASTER *Aster divaricatus* L.

This dry-woodland perennial grows to a height of 1 to 2 feet. The leaves have fairly long slender petioles and are 1 to 5 inches long. The heads bear 6 to 10 white ray-flowers (sometimes tinted with rose) and measure a scant inch across. The involucral bracts are broad.

There are so many species of Asters and much regional variation that the exact determination of a specimen may often be debatable.

Figure 418

3a At least the branches of the inflorescence with large glands; ray-flowers usually 3 toothed, violet. Fig. 419.

LARGE LEAVED ASTER *Aster macrophyllus* L.

This broad, rough-leaved, reddish-stemmed plant grows in dry soil and becomes 2 to 3 feet high. The leaves are thick, the lower ones with long petioles. The heads are about an inch broad and bear 12 to 18 lavender or violet rays.

Figure 419

3b Plants not all glandular. 4

4a At least some of the stem leaves expanded at the base into a heart-shaped clasping arrangement (a); flowers pale blue to violet. Fig. 420. **WAVY-LEAF ASTER** *Aster undulatus* **L.**

Stem pubescent, stiff and very rough, 1 to 3 feet high. Leaves thick, rough on both sides, pubescent beneath; the lower ones 2-6 inches long; those of the stem clasping at their base. Rays 8 to 16, violet or pale blue. It grows in dry soil.

Figure 420

4b None of the stem leaves with heart-shaped clasping device.......**5**

5a Most of the leaves thin and with sharply serrate margins. Fig. 421. ....**7**

Figure 421

5b Leaves thick; margins wholly entire or nearly so. Fig. 422. ....**6**

Figure 422

6a Upper surface of leaves smooth, or nearly so. Fig. 423.
SHORT'S ASTER *Aster shortii* **Hook**

Two to 4 feet high. The leaves are 2 to 6 inches long and 1 to 2 inches wide, usually entire but part of them sometimes with small teeth. Upper leaves lanceolate, sessile or short petioled. Heads numerous in open panicles, the rays 10-16, bluish-violet.

Figure 423

6b Upper surface of leaves rough; much longer than wide. Fig. 424.
SKY-BLUE ASTER *Aster azureus* **Lindl.**

This slender-stemmed plant attains a height of 1 to 4 feet; it is much branched above. The leaves are scabrous on both sides, the lower ones measuring 2 to 6 inches long; the upper leaves are linear and usually sessile. The many heads are in loose panicles; the bright blue rays number 10 to 20; the achenes have a tawny pappus. It grows at the border of woods and open prairies.

Figure 424

7a Involucre ¼ inch or less high, the bracts mostly obtuse, appressed and with colored tips. Fig. 425.
COMMON BLUE WOOD ASTER *Aster cordifolius* **L.**

This practically glabrous perennial grows to a height of 1 to 5 feet. The leaves are 2 to 6 inches long, the blades being rather thick and the lower leaves with slender petioles. The heads are up to 1 inch across and have 12 to 20 light blue rays, with white pappus. It grows in rich soil.

Figure 425

7b Involucre usually more than ¼ inch high, the bracts are loosely attached and with tips uncolored. 8

8a Stems and underside of leaves densely covered with short, white woolly pubescence, petioles usually winged. Fig. 426.
DRUMMOND'S ASTER *Aster sagittifolius drummondii* **Lindl.**

This rather straggling plant grows in open woods and fields to a height of 1 to 4 feet. The leaves are 2 to 4 inches long and rather thin. The 8 to 15 rays are blue, usually pale, the pappus white and the heads about 2/3 inch across. It is a rather easily recognized species.

Figure 426

8b Leaves green beneath; stems smooth or but slightly hairy.
Fig. 427.   ARROW-LEAVED ASTER *Aster sagittifolius* Willd.

This aster grows to a height of 2 to 5 feet and prefers dry soil. The upper leaves are lanceolate and usually sessile, though sometimes with petioles; the lower leaves measure 3 to 6 inches long and are cordate and petiolate. The 10 to 16 purplish or pale blue rays make the heads a bit less than an inch across.

Figure 427

9a Stem leaves with clasping base, often heart-shaped. 10

9b Stem leaves with narrow base, not clasping. 15

10a Involucre with glandular hairs; flowers deep purple usually 1 inch or more across. Fig. 428.
NEW ENGLAND ASTER *Aster novae-angliae* L.

This heavy-stemmed erect plant grows to a height of 2 to 10 feet or even more. The leaves are 2 to 5 inches long and usually rather less than an inch wide; the base if definitely clasping. The involucral bracts are spreading and somewhat spatulate. The heads are numerous with 40 to 50 usually deep violet-purple rays and may attain a width of 2 inches. The pappus is pink-tinged and the achenes pubescent.

It grows along road sides, in fields and especially in wet places. It is frequently cultivated and may display white, pink or red flowers.

Figure 428

10b Involucre without glands. 11

11a Bracts of involucre of several different lengths, leaves usually entire or with but scattered serrations. 14

11b Bracts of involucre about equal in length and tapering to a point. 12

12a All of the leaves entire, rather broadly wedge-shaped and auriculate-clasping. Fig. 429.   LATE PURPLE ASTER *Aster patens* **Ait.**

Figure 429

This slender-stemmed plant (1 to 3 feet high) is widely scattered in dry, open places. The leaves, often with obtuse tips, are 1 to 3 inches long, the top-most ones being but tiny bract-like structures. The heads, 1 inch or more across, have 20 to 30 deep violet or bluish-purple rays; the achenes are pubescent and the pappus pale brown.

12b Most of the leaves with serrate margins. 13

13a Leaves narrowing below middle, then expanding into a wide clasping base. Fig. 430.

CROOKED-STEM ASTER *Aster prenanthoides* **Muhl.**

Figure 430

This small much-branched aster is found in moist soil and has a height of 1 to 2 feet. The thin leaves range from 3 to 8 inches in length; the larger ones being 1½ inches wide and wrap their base around the stem; 20 to 30 violet rays make a head about 1 inch across. The involucral bracts are spreading; the pappus is tawny and the achenes pubescent.

13b Leaves gently tapering to a narrow but clasping base. Fig. 431.
RED-STALK ASTER *Aster puniceus* L.

This sturdy-growing glabrous-to-hispid plant, lives in wet places and has a height of 3 to 8 feet. The leaves are often much roughened above; they may be an inch or more wide with a length up to 6 inches. The 20 to 40 pale to darker violet rays form the often numerous heads an inch or more wide.

This as well as many of the other asters is quite variable, which feature, combined with the large numbers, both of species and of individuals, offers many chances for uncertainty.

Figure 431

14a Leaves narrow lanceolate; suddenly constricting near the base, then widening into a small clasping structure. Fig. 432.
NEW YORK ASTER *Aster novi-belgii* L.

This slender stemmed plant grows to a height of 1 to 3 feet. The usually glabrous leaves are slender lanceolate, firm and but slightly if at all serrate; they measure 2 to 6 inches in length and ¼ to a little more than ½ inch wide. The heads with 15 to 25 violet rays measure about ¾ inch across. The achenes are smooth with white pappus.

Figure 432

14b Leaves broader and usually oval at the wider clasping base. Fig. 433.
SMOOTH ASTER *Aster laevis* L.

This sturdy aster has a height of 2 to 4 feet. The leaves are 1 to 5 inches long and up to 2 inches wide; they are thick and often broadly cordate-clasping. The violet or blue rays are 15 to 30 in heads about 1 inch broad. The achenes are smooth with a tawny pappus.

Figure 433

15a Leaves thickened, fleshy, slender and entire; plants growing in salty areas. 16

15b Plants not as in 15a. 17

16a Heads ½ inch or more across; perennial. Fig. 434.
PERENNIAL SALT-MARSH ASTER *Aster tenuifolius* L.

Figure 434

This smooth fleshy plant grows in salty coastal areas and has a height of 1 to 2 feet. The lower leaves are linear, often clasping and 2 to 6 inches long; the upper ones are short. The few heads are ½ to 1 inch broad with many purple or sometimes whitish rays; the pappus is tawny.

16b Heads less than ½ inch broad; annual. Fig. 435.
ANNUAL SALT-MARSH ASTER *Aster subulatus* Michx.

Figure 435

This smooth fleshy annual grows to a height of 1 to 5 feet and is found in salty areas along the Atlantic coast. The leaves are 2 to 10 inches long; the heads are ¼ to less than ½ inch and have 20 to 30 purple rays. The pappus is whitish.

17a Leaves covered on both sides with a silvery pubescence.
Fig. 436.   **EASTERN SILVERY ASTER** *Aster concolor* L.

Figure 436

This slender plant grows in dry sandy soil mostly near the coast and may attain a height of 2 feet or more. The larger leaves are about 2 inches long. The heads are ¾ to nearly an inch across and bear 10 to 15 lilac rays.

WESTERN SILVERY ASTER *A. sericeus* Vent., grows in dry soil throughout much of the Middle West. Its larger flowers have 15 to 25 violet-blue rays. The leaves are covered with silvery hairs. It stands around 2 feet. The achenes are smooth instead of hairy as in *concolor*.

17b Leaves not silvery. 18
18a Involucre with glandular hairs.. Basal leaves much larger than
the stem leaves and with definite and usually long petioles.
Fig. 437.   **LOW SHOWY ASTER** *Aster spectabilis* Ait.

Figure 437

This plant has a height of 1 to 2 feet. It grows in dry soil, its stiff stem being 1 to 2 feet high. The upper leaves are sessile; the lower ones have slender petioles and may be 5 inches long. The heads are over an inch across and have 20 to 30 bright violet rays. The pappus is whitish.

18b Involucre without glands; not sticky; lower leaves without conspicuous petioles. 19

19a Leaves arising from the stem, linear. Fig. 438. ...20

Figure 438

19b Stem-leaves broader. Fig. 439. 26

Figure 439

20a Stem very pubescent or roughened; both leaves and heads crowded; heads about ¼ inch across. Fig. 440.
          DENSE-FLOWERED ASTER *Aster ericoides prostratus* (Ktze.)

Figure 440

This plant, both interesting and decorative, has a stem length of 1 to 5 feet; often low and spreading. The many narrow leaves are ½ to 1½ inches long and somewhat clasping. The heads are ¼ to 1/3 inch across and have 10 to 20 white rays. It grows in dry places.

WHITE PRAIRIE ASTER *A. commutatus* (T. & G.), growing from Minnesota to Texas, is similar to the above but has larger heads with more rays (20 to 30).

165

20b Stem at most but slightly pubescent and otherwise also not as in 20a. 21

21a Involucre 1/5 inch or less in height, rays white. 22

21b Involucre more than 1/5 inch high. 24

22a Bracts with sturdy awl-shaped tip; involucre as wide as high, (campanulate or hemispherical). Fig. 441.

WHITE HEATH ASTER *Aster ericoides* L.

Figure 441

Known also as Frost Aster and Michaelmas Daisy it grows in dry soil and has a height of 2 to 3 feet. Its rather stiff leaves are 1 to 3 inches long. The 15 to 25 brilliant white rays (occasionally tinged with reddish) are borne in heads 1/3 to ½ inch or more across. The achenes bear a fine pubescence and the pappus is white. It continues flowering later than many of the asters.

22b Bracts without stiff awl-shaped tips. 23

23a Bracts with conspicuous broadened green tips; heads up to 1 inch broad; rays usually violet or purplish. Occasional specimens might seem to fall here. (See Fig. 449).

WILLOW ASTER *Aster praealtus* Poir.

23b Bracts without broadened tips; head ½ inch or a bit broader; rays white or whitish. Fig. 442.

TRADESCANT'S ASTER *Aster tradescanti* L.

Figure 442

It grows with ascending branches, in fields and wet places, to a height of 2 to 5 feet. The usually narrow stem leaves (occasionally lanceolate) have a length of 3 to 6 inches and range from entire to moderately serrate. The heads have many white rays; the pappus is white.

24a None of the leaves as much as 2 inches long; rays 10 to 15, usually violet. Fig. 443.

STIFF-LEAVED ASTER *Aster linariifolius* L.

This low branching perennial seldom has a height over 2 feet, often less. The linear leaves (occasionally spatulate) are stiff and rough and measure up to 1½ inches long. The heads are about an inch broad; the rays (rarely white) are violet. The tawny pappus is in two circles, the outer hairs being very short. Sand-paper Starwort is a descriptive name.

Figure 443

24b Many of the leaves over 2 inches in length. 25

25a Annual with very small heads and short purplish rays. (See Fig. 435 as that plant might seem to fall here).

ANNUAL SALT-MARSH ASTER *Aster subulatus* Michx.

25b Tall perennial with numerous heads ¾ inch or broader, rays white. (See Fig. 448 as some specimens of that species might seem to belong here).

TALL WHITE ASTER *Aster simplex* Willd.

26a Heads in racemes or panicles. 28

26b Heads in flat-topped corymbs, rays white. 27

27a Leaves rather broadly lanceolate, usually entire; pappus in two circles, the other short (a). Fig. 444.

TALL FLAT-TOP WHITE ASTER *Aster umbellatus* Mill.

Its glabrous (sometimes pubescent) stem has a height of 1 to 8 feet, with stem leaves up to 6 inches long and an inch wide. The many heads measure in breadth from ½ inch to nearly an inch and have 10 to 15 white rays. The pappus is white and double. It grows in moist areas.

Figure 444

27b Leaves narrower, as pictured, stiff; pappus in but one circle of equal-lengthed parts (a). Fig. 445.

UPLAND WHITE ASTER *Aster ptarmicoides* (Nees.)

This stiff rough plant grows to a height of 1 to 2 feet. The 1 to 3 ribbed leaves are usually entire with a possible length of 6 inches and 1/3 inch wide. The heads an inch or a little less across have 10 to 20 white rays. The simple pappus is white and the achenes smooth. It is found in dry soil.

Figure 445

28a Stems with distinct coat of pubescence. 29

28b Stems glabrous or practically so. 31

29a Heads 1 inch or more broad. Fig. 446.

WHORLED ASTER *Aster acuminatus* Michx.

This pubescent, zigzag plant stands 1 to 3 feet high and grows in moist woods. The leaves are pubescent beneath and often also on the upper surface; they measure 3 to 6 inches and may be 1½ inches wide. The heads are from an inch to 1½ inches wide and bear 12 to 20 white or purplish rays. The pubescent achenes bear white pappus.

Figure 446

29b Heads less than 1 inch broad. 30

168

30a Leaves lanceolate with prominent serrations; heads in a one-sided raceme; disk flowers turning reddish. Fig. 447.

CALICO ASTER *Aster lateriflorus* (L.)

This very common, often reclining, species has a stem length of 1 to 4 feet or more. The basal leaves have slender petioles but those of the stem are sessile and fairly broad. The heads are a bit under ½ inch in width and numerous in the arching racemes. The ray-flowers are many and white or pale lavender. The disk-flowers are purplish or reddish, depending upon their age. This is a rather highly variable species and is widely distributed.

Figure 447

30b Heads in panicles; leaves rather narrow and long; heads about ¾ inch broad, rays white. (See Fig. 448 as some specimens of this variable species could key to here).

TALL WHITE ASTER *Aster simplex* Willd.

31a Annual, growing in salty areas, fleshy, heads small. (See Fig. 435).   ANNUAL SALT-MARSH ASTER *Aster subulatus* Michx.

31b Not as in 31a. 32

32a Heads in ascending panicles. 33

32b Heads in 1-sided racemes. (See Fig. 447).

CALICO ASTER *Aster lateriflorus* (L.)

33a Heads but little if any over ½ inch broad; rays usually white. (See Fig. 442).   TRADESCANT'S ASTER *Aster tradescanti* L.

33b Heads larger, ¾ inch or more across. .34

34a Leaves thin and rather smooth; involucral bracts tapering to a point; rays white or pale violet. Fig. 448.

FALL WHITE ASTER *Aster simplex* Willd.

This usually glabrous-stemmed perennial grows to a height of 2 to 8 feet. The leaves are mostly serrate but sometimes entire and have a length of 3 to 6 inches and are up to ½ inch wide. The numerous heads have a short involucre of appressed green-tipped bract; the rays are white or pale violet, while the finely pubescent achenes bear white pappus.

It is a rather highly variable species growing in moist soil.

Figure 448

169

34b Leaves thicker, stiff and roughened; involucral bracts acute or obtuse, angular pointed; rays usually purplish or violet. Fig. 449.
WILLOW ASTER *Aster praealtus* Poir.

Figure 449

This is a very leafy plant attaining a height of 2 to 5 feet. The leaves, often somewhat clasping at the base, have a maximum length of 4 inches and width of ½ inch, and may be either serrate or entire margined. The many heads have a width up to 1 inch. The numerous rays are occasionally white but usually violet or purplish. The pubescent achenes bear a white pappus. The species varies considerably; it grows in moist soil.

GOLDEN-RODS Genus Solidago

1a Rays more numerous than the disk-flowers; heads sessile or nearly so; leaves narrow and entire; receptacle flattened with a hair-like fringe (a). Fig. 450. 2

Figure 450

1b Ray-flowers usually fewer than the disk-flowers; heads usually with stems, not sessile; receptacle pitted. 3

2a Leaves with but one rib (principal vein); heads with less than 20 flowers. Fig. 451.
SLENDER FRAGRANT GOLDEN-ROD *Solidago tenuifolia* Pursh

Figure 451

This is a low resinous plant often but little over a foot high. The grass-like leaves are up to 3 inches long and about ⅛ inch wide. The tiny heads are crowded in a flat-topped inflorescence. The 4 to 7 disk flowers are surrounded by 6 to 14 ray-flowers.

NARROW-LEAVED BUSHY GOLDEN-ROD S. *microcephala* (Greene), a taller and still narrower-leaved plant grows in dry sandy places from Virginia and Mississippi to Florida.

2b Leaves with 3 to 5 ribs; heads with 20 or more flowers. Fig. 452.
BUSHY GOLDEN-ROD *Solidago graminifolia* (L.)

Figure 452

This moist-soil species attains a height of 2 to 3 feet or more and has a much branched bushy growth. The 3 to 5 veined leaves up to 5 inches long and 1/3 inch wide. The heads are a little less than ¼ inch high and have 12 to 18 rays and 8 to 12 disk-flowers.

SMALL-HEADED BUSHY GOLDEN-ROD *S. floribunda* (Greene), an eastern species has smaller heads and greenish involucral bracts instead of yellowish.

3a Rays yellow. **4**

3b Rays white (or cream-colored); plants with heavy gray pubescence.
Fig. 453. **WHITE GOLDEN-ROD** *Solidago bicolor* L.

Figure 453

This Silver-rod or Silver-weed, as it is sometimes called, grows in dry soil and has a height up to 3 feet or more. The leaves are thickly covered with whitish hairs and measure 2 to 4 inches with an occasional width of nearly 2 inches. The heads are in small groups in the axil of the leaves; the achenes are glabrous.

4a Bracts of involucre (a) erect and appressed; tips not green. Fig. 454. ....**5**

Figure 454

4b Involucral bracts with green tips, which spread outward and often turn downward. Fig. 455.

STOUT RAGGED GOLDEN-ROD *Solidago squarrosa* Muhl.

The upper leaves of this 2-to-5-foot plant are often entire but the lower ones are broadly oval and sharply toothed. They measure 5 to 10 inches long and up to 3 inches wide. The heads have 8 to 16 rays and 12 to 25 disk flowers.

DOWNY RAGGED GOLDEN-ROD *S. petolaris* Ait., ranging from North Carolina to Kansas and southward, is similar but has smaller, roughly-ciliated leaves.

Figure 455

5a (a, b, c, d) Heads in a flat-topped inflorescence; leaves thick, stiff and often clasping and entire. Fig. 456.

STIFF-LEAVED GOLDEN-ROD *Solidago rigida* L.

This easily recognized hoary species has a height of 1 to 5 feet; it grows in poor dry soil. Most of the leaves are sessile and clasping but the basal ones have a long petiole giving a total length of 10 inches or more. The 6 to 10 rays are large and give the heads a ragged appearance.

Figure 456

5b Heads in a spike-like arrangement or scattered in clusters along the stem as in Figs. 457 to 459. 6

5c Head in a terminal spreading panicle, frequently with recurving branches. (See Figs. 462 to 472). 9

5d Heads in a rather compact panicle (See Figs. 460 and 461). 8

6a Plant heavily pubescent. Fig. 457.

HAIRY GOLDEN-ROD *Solidago hispida* Muhl.

This very hairy plant grows ruggedly to a height of nearly 3 feet. The leaves are pubescent on both sides; the lower ones are petioled and up to 5 inches long; the upper leaves are sessile. The involucral bracts are yellow; the heads are about ¼ inch high and often crowded in axillary clusters. It prefers dry soil.

Figure 457

6b Stems and leaves glabrous or mostly so. 7

7a Leaves lanceolate to oblong; stem round in cross-section. Fig. 458.

BLUE-STEMMED GOLDEN-ROD *Solidago caesia* L.

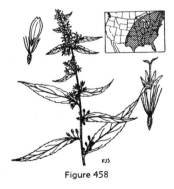

In keeping with its name, this species may be recognized by its bluish or purplish stem. The heads are scattered along the stem in little clusters as pictured and are ¼ inch or less high. The plant grows up to 3 feet. Its lanceolate leaves (broader below) are 2 to **five** inches and glabrous. It is found in woods and protected places.

Figure 458

7b Leaves broadly oval with margined petioles; stems irregular with grooves and angles in cross-section. Fig. 459.

BROAD-LEAVED GOLDEN-ROD *Solidago flexicaulis* L.

This plant often grows with a zig-zag stem (1 to 3 feet) and is known as the Zig-Zag Golden-rod. The leaves are thin and many of them with petioles. They are up to 6 inches long and as much as 3 inches wide. The heads are about ¼ inch high. It, too, is a woods plant.

CURTIS' GOLDEN-ROD *S. curtisii* T. & G., is a quite similar southern species; its leaves are narrower and sessile. It ranges from Virginia and Kentucky southward.

Figure 459

8a Stem usually downy; involucral bracts sharply acute. Fig. 460.

DOWNY GOLDEN-ROD *Solidago puberula* Nutt.

This usually slender species has a height of some 3 feet with sessile lanceolate stem-leaves up to 2 inches long. The basal leaves have petioles and are 2 to 4 inches in length. It grows in sandy soil and is sometimes glabrous. The student of systematic botany soon learns that plant characters are not always as stable as he might wish.

Figure 460

8b Stem glabrous, often roughened above; involucral bracts very obtuse. Fig. 461. SHOWY GOLDEN-ROD *Solidago speciosa* Nutt.

This sturdy-growing golden-rod grows up to 7 feet high and bears its flowering heads in profusion. The leaves are 4 to 10 inches long and up to 4 inches wide; the achenes are smooth or practically so. The heads are about 1/3 inch tall.

Figure 461

9a Leaves fleshy, entire; growing in salt-marshes and along sea-beaches. Fig. 462.

SEA-SIDE GOLDEN-ROD *Solidago sempervirens* L.

Figure 462

This sturdily growing plant lives in salt-water areas, sea coasts, tidal-river banks, salt marshes, etc. and has a height up to 8 feet. The leaves are fleshy, entire; the upper ones are sessile, while the lower leaves are sometimes petioled and nearly a foot long. The heads may be close to ½ inch high; with 8 to 12 showy rays.

9b Not as in 9a. 10

10a Leaves with 3 longitudinal veins. Fig. 463. 14

Figure 463

10b Leaves pinnately veined. Fig. 464. 11

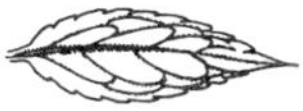

Figure 464

11a Stem heavily pubescent; leaves sharply serrate and usually pubescent. Fig. 465.

TALL HAIRY GOLDEN-ROD *Solidago rugosa* Mill.

Figure 465

This is a high growing (1 to 7 feet), strongly pubescent species, with leaves 2 to 4 inches long and up to 1½ inches in width; they are usually sharply serrate. The heads are small, the involucre cylindrical, with but few bracts. It grows in dry soil and in woodlands. It is highly variable and is a very common species.

11b Stem glabrous or mostly so. 12

12a Leaves very rough on the upper side. Fig. 466.
ROUGH LEAVED GOLDEN-ROD *Solidago patula* Muhl.

This is another tall golden-rod. It grows in wet areas and may attain a height of 7 feet. The lower leaves may be nearly ½ foot wide, have long petioles and are some-times over a foot long. The heads are about ¼ inch high and possess small inconspic-uous rays.

Figure 466

12b Leaves smooth or but slightly roughened above. 13

13a Panicle with but few branches; leaves thin and coarsely serrate. Fig. 467. ELM-LEAVED GOLDEN-ROD *Solidago ulmifolia* Muhl.

This often glabrous-stemmed plant grows in woods and thickets to a height of 2 to 4 feet. The leaves are thin, sparingly pubescent and the upper ones nearly sessile, while the lower ones have rather long, margined petioles and are up to 5 inches long. The deep-yellow rays are fewer than in many species.

Figure 467

13b Panicle with many branches; spreading and often recurved; leaves lanceolate, firm. Fig. 468.
SHARP-TOOTHED GOLDEN-ROD *Solidago juncea* Ait.

This smooth-stemmed plant may stand up to 4 feet in height. It grows in dry places and produces stiff sessile stem leaves, both serrate and entire and rather long petioled basal leaves with a length up to a foot. The heads are small and bear 7 to 12 rays. The branches of the panicle are often long and recurving.

Figure 468

14a Head numerous but very small, 1/10 inch high or less; leaves thin, narrowly lanceolate. Fig. 469.

CANADA GOLDEN-ROD *Solidago canadensis* L.

Figure 469

This widely distributed and highly variable plant has a height of 1 to 5 feet. The linear-lanceolate leaves bear sharp serrations and are 2 to 5 inches long. The heads are tiny, very numerous in the large panicle and have but few short rays (4 to 6).

14b Heads ⅛ to ¼ inch high. 15

15a Stem covered with pubescence or roughened with scales. 16

15b Stem smooth, glabrous; leaves thin. Fig. 470.

LATE GOLDEN-ROD *Solidago gigantea* Ait.

Figure 470

This sturdy moist-soil species grows to a height of 3 to 7 feet. The stems are glabrous and sometimes with a glaucous bloom. The 3 to 6 inch leaves (sometimes more than an inch wide) are three-nerved and sessile. The heads are about ¼ inch high and develop 8 to 16 fairly long rays. The achenes are covered with a fine pubescence.

16a Leaves broadest near outer end (spatulate or ob-lanceolate); ashy-gray with dense pubescence. Fig. 471.

GRAY GOLDEN-ROD *Solidago nemoralis* Ait.

Figure 471

This smaller golden-rod grows to a height of 6 to 20 inches. The fine pubescence gives the thick plant a gray appearance. The leaves are 3 to 6 inches long; the heads usually less than ¼ inch high, and have 5 to 10 yellow rays. The achenes are pubescent. It grows in dry soil and ranges widely.

16b Leaves lanceolate, rough as above. Fig. 472.

DOUBLE GOLDEN-ROD *Solidago altissima* L.

Figure472

This 2 to 8 foot sturdy plant has more ray flowers per head than is usual (up to 16 or more), which accounts for its "Double" name. The leaves are 3 nerved, 3 to 6 inches long and up to 1 inch wide. The heads are less than ¼ inch high and have 5 to 9 rays. The achenes are pubescent. It is a dry-soil plant.

SPANISH NEEDLES Genus Bidens

1a Aquatic, with very finely dissected leaves under water but a few broad-bladed leaves and the flowering heads standing above water. Fig. 473.

WATER MARIGOLD *Bidens beckii* Torr.

Figure 473

Stems 2 to 8 feet long, growing mostly submerged with sessile, finely-divided leaves, as pictured. The 6 to 10 rayed heads about 1½ inch across are a rich yellow and stand above water with a few broadened leaves an inch or more long. The seeds bear several slender, barbed awns. It grows in ponds and streams.

1b Normal terrestrial plants. 2

2a Ray-flowers absent, rudimentary or very short. (See Figs. 476 to 479). 3

2b Ray-flowers conspicuous. (See Fig. 481). 6

3a Leaves pinnately divided. Fig. 474. 4

Figure 474

3b Leaves mostly lanceolate. Fig. 475. 5

Figure 475

4a Achenes ("seeds") linear (a). Fig. 476.

SPANISH NEEDLES *Bidens bipinnata* L.

Figure 476

This square-stemmed annual grows in rich soil to a height of 1 to 6 feet. The 1 to 3-times dissected leaves are thin and may attain a length of 8 inches. The numerous heads are borne on long slender stems. The yellow rays are 3 to 4 or even none and short and inconspicuous. The seeds measure a good half inch and usually bear 4 diverging, barbed awns.

4b Achenes ("seeds") flat (a). Fig. 477.

BEGGAR-TICKS *Bidens frondosa* L.

Figure 477

This usually purplish stemmed annual has a height of 2 to 3 feet. The leaves are 3 to 5 divided and thin, with slender petioles. There are usually no ray flowers; if present, weak and inconspicuous. The heads of yellow disk flowers are surrounded by 4 to 8 slender green bracts and several shorter, inner ones. The achenes are blackish and have two awns. It is an all-too-common weed in moist soil.

179

5a Heads always erect; disk-flowers orange, stems purple. Fig. 478.
PURPLE-STEMMED SWAMP BEGGAR-TICK *Bidens connata* Muhl.

Figure 478

This European introduced weed is now widely scattered in swamps and wet soil. The purple stems stand 1 to 8 feet high. The thin coarsely-serrated leaves are 2 to 5 inches long and petioled. The ray-flowers are few and inconspicuous or absent; the disk-flowers are orange. The flattened achenes have usually 2 (sometimes 4) rather long awns and have won for the plant the name "Pitchforks".

5b Heads nodding after the flowers mature; leaves sessile or united at their base; rays if present shorter than the bracts of the involucre. Fig. 479.   **NODDING BUR-MARIGOLD** *Bidens cernua* L.

Figure 479

This annual grows to a possible height of 3 feet. The sessile leaves may have a width of 1 inch and are 3 - 6 inches long. The heads are globular and numerous. The 6 to 10 rays are short or sometimes entirely missing. The heads are hemispherical. The wedge-shaped achenes usually have 4 awns. It is a wet soil plant and is widely distributed.

6a Leaves mostly pinnately divided. Fig. 480. 7

Figure 480

6b **Leaves lanceolate. Fig. 481.**

LARGER BUR-MARIGOLD *Bidens laevis* **(L.)**

Figure 481

This glabrous annual has a height of 1 to 3 feet. The opposite, sessile, serrate leaves are 3 to 8 inches long and up to 1 inch wide. The many golden-yellow heads are borne on short stems and have a width of 1 to 2½ inches and bear 7 to 10 broad ray-flowers. The achenes have two rather long slender awns and sometimes two shorter ones. It grows in low wet places.

7a **Achenes with 2 short teeth as pictured (a); achenes with but some short pubescence. Fig. 482.**

SOUTHERN TICKSEED-SUNFLOWER *Bidens coronata* **(L.)**

Figure 482

This glabrous annual grows in wet places and has a height of 1 to 3 feet. The upper leaves are small, narrow and sometimes 3 lobed; the lower ones may be as much as 5 inches long and are usually 3-parted with fairly long petioles. It is a prolific bloomer; the deep yellow heads of 6 to 10 broad rays measure 1 to 2 inches across.

7b **Achenes with longer, more slender awns, and with long pubescence. Fig. 483. ....8**

Figure 483

8a **Achenes much flattened, awns 2 to 4, nearly as long as the achene. Fig. 484.**

WESTERN TICKSEED-SUNFLOWER *Bidens aristosa* **(Michx.)**

Figure 484

This plant grows in wet places and has a height of 1 to 3 feet. It is often a biennal. The thin, 5 to 7-divided leaves are up to 6 inches long. The flowering heads may be 2 inches across and bear 6 to 10 rather broad yellow rays. The barbed awns are sometimes absent.

The several members of this genus give great brilliancy to our fall landscapes.

181

8b Achenes wedge-shaped or somewhat linear and bearing ciliated ear-like awns as pictured (a). Fig. 485.

TALL TICKSEED-SUNFLOWER *Bidens coronata trichosperma* (Michx.)

This somewhat square-stemmed sturdy perennial (or sometimes annual) has a height of 2 to 5 feet. The leaves, sometimes 8 inches long, are 5 to 7 divided. The 6 to 18 golden yellow rays make up the numerous conspicuous heads some 2 inches across. The achene bears 2 diverging hispid teeth. Like most of the members of the genus, it grows in wet places.

Figure 485

SUNFLOWERS Genus Helianthus

1a Disk dark brown or purplish, *(H. annuus,* has a yellowish disk in some cultivated varieties). Upper leaves alternate. 2

1b Disk yellow or yellowish. 3

2a Leaves linear or linear-lanceolate, sessile; heads 2 to 3 inches broad. Fig. 486.

NARROW-LEAVED SUNFLOWER *Helianthus angustifolius* L.

This swamp-loving perennial grows to a height of 2 to 7 feet. The leaves have a length of 2 to 8 inches and are sessile, entire and firm and usually fairly smooth. The heads are few and have a hemispherical purplish disk in contrast to the flattened one of the Common Sunflower. There are 12 to 20 yellow rays. It is most common near the coast.

Figure 486

2b Leaves ovate, petioled; heads 3 - 6 inches broad (some cultivated varieties much broader). Annual. Fig. 487.

COMMON SUNFLOWER *Helianthus annuus* L.

Figure 487

This well-known state flower of Kansas, grows native on the prairies from Minnesota and North Dakota to Texas and California. This native form has a height of 3 to 7 feet with broad rough leaves becoming a foot or more in length. There are many cultivated varieties raised over a wide area (and often escaped) as ornamentals, or for forage, seeds, fibre, honey, oil, etc. These cultigens may be "double" (all ray flowers); with rays striped with red or wholly so; with great disks producing large quantities of seeds; and other interesting variations, and may attain a height of 15 feet or more.

3a (a, b, c) Disk about ¼ inch broad; heads 1 to 1½ inches across; leaves oblong-lanceolate, very thin and delicate. Fig. 488.

SMALL WOOD SUNFLOWER *Helianthus microcephalus* T. & G.

Figure 488

This slender, sparingly branched, smooth little perennial grows in damp woods and along streams to a height of 3 to 6 feet. The leaves are ovate-lanceolate to lanceolate, rough above and mostly opposite, 3 to 7 inches long. The sometimes numerous heads are borne on long slender stems; there are 5 - 10 rays; the chaff is 3-toothed or sometimes entire. The seeds usually bear 2 small awns.

183

3b Disk ¼ to ⅝ inches broad; leaves broader and very thin, opposite.
    Fig. 489.   **THIN-LEAVED SUNFLOWER** *Helianthus decapetalus* L.

Figure 489

Its slender, usually glabrous stems attain a height of 2 to 5 feet. The thin leaves have a length of 3 to 8 inches and a width of 1 to 3 inches. The heads are numerous and 2 to 3 inches across. The 8 to 15 light yellow rays surround a flattened yellow disk. The glabrous seeds have two scale-like awns and are interspersed with entire to 3-toothed chaff. It grows in moist places especially in the woods.

3c Disk ⅜ to 1¼ inches or more across; leaves mostly firm. 4

4a Leaves narrowly lanceolate. 5

4b Leaves broadly lanceolate to ovate. 6

5a Leaves sessile or nearly so; stem rough-hairy, at least above.
    Fig. 490.   **GIANT SUNFLOWER** *Helianthus giganteus* L.

Figure 490

The usually purple stems attain a height of 3 to 12 feet; the leaves are very rough above and 2 to 6 inches long but seldom over 1 inch wide. The usually several heads, have 10 to 20 rays and may attain a width of nearly 3 inches. The pappus consists of but two awns. It grows in swamps and wet fields.

5b Leaves long petioled (1½ to 3¼ inches long); stem smooth and waxy. Fig. 491.

SAW-TOOTHED SUNFLOWER *Helianthus grosse-serratus* Martens

Figure 491

This sturdy perennial attains a height of 5 to 10 feet. The leaves may attain a length of 8 inches and have slender definite petioles. They are usually rather coarsely and sharply serrate. The heads are up to 3 inches broad and have 10 to 20 deep yellow rays. It is widely distributed in dry soil.

6a Stem rough-hairy; leaves ovate; ray flowers 12 to 20. 7

6b Stem smooth, at least below; leaves broadly lanceolate and usually opposite; rays 8 - 15. ....8 ·

7a Leaves sessile or clasping at their base; plant 2 to 3½ feet high; disk ¾ to 1¼ inch across. Fig. 492.

HAIRY SUNFLOWER *Helianthus mollis* Lam.

This rugged perennial grows to a height of 2 to 4 feet in dry soil; as the name suggests it is densely hirsuit, 2 to 5 inches long and up to nearly 3 inches broad. The 18 to 25 ray flowers surround a yellow disk. The achenes are usually smooth.

FJS

Figure 492

7b Leaves with long petioles; plant 3 - 9 feet high; disk ½ inch broad.
Fig. 493.   JERUSALEM ARTICHOKE *Helianthus tuberosus* **L.**

This attractive plant grows to a height of 7 to 12 feet, from thick heavy tubers, which are frequently eaten and could well be more largely used in this way. The Indians likely widened its range through their cultivation of the plant. The sturdy, three-nerved leaves attain a length of 4 to 8 inches. The flowering heads bear 12 to 20 bright yellow rays and measure 2 to 3½ inches across; the seeds are pubescent.

Figure 493

8a Ray flowers ¾ inches long; leaves rough on both sides and spreading. Fig. 494.   ROUGH SUNFLOWER *Helianthus divaricatus* **L.**

The usually wholly glabrous stem grows to a height of 3 to 7 feet. The leaves are up to 1½ inches wide and 8 inches long. The flowering heads have a width of about 2 inches and are often solitary. There are 8-15 ray flowers surrounding a yellow disk. The chaff is deeply 3 lobed and the seeds smooth. It grows in dry shady places.

Figure 494

8b Ray flowers 1 to 1½ inches long; leaves whitish beneath and abruptly rounded to a short petiole. Fig. 495.
PALE-LEAVED WOOD SUNFLOWER *Helianthus strumosus* **L.**

This often tuberous-rooted perennial grows 3 - 7 feet high. The leaves 3 - 8 inches long have short petioles and are rough above but with a whitish pubescence beneath. The heads have a width of 3 to 4 inches and bear 6 to 15 ray flowers. The seeds are glabrous but the chaff pubescent.

Figure 495

186

A CHECK LIST OF THE GENERA IN THEIR LOGICAL ORDER BY FAMILIES

The generic names which follow represent the plants treated in this book. They are arranged here by families for checking and reference.

MONOCOTYLEDONS p. 16

CAT-TAIL FAMILY Typhaceae
Typha p. 17
PONDWEED FAMILY Najadaceae
Potamogeton p. 16
ARROW GRASS FAMILY Juncaginaceae
Triglochin p. 17
WATER-PLANTAIN FAMILY Alismaceae
Sagittaria p. 18, 19
Alisma p. 18
FROG'S BIT FAMILY Hydrocharitaceae
Vallisneria p. 25
PIPEWORT FAMILY Ericaulaceae
Eriocaulon p. 21
YELLOW-EYED GRASS FAMILY Xyridaceae
Xyris p. 20
SPIDERWORT FAMILY Commelinaceae
Commelina p. 23

PICKEREL-WEED FAMILY Pontederiaceae
Pontederia p. 22
Heteranthera p. 22

LILY FAMILY Liliaceae
Stenanthium p. 24
Melanthium p. 24
Allium p. 23

BLOODWORT FAMILY Haemodoraceae
Lachnanthes p. 26

AMARYLLIS FAMILY Amaryllidaceae
Hymenocallis p. 25

ORCHID FAMILY Orchidaceae
Habenaria p. 27
Triphora p. 27
Spiranthes p. 28-30
Goodyera p. 28
Corallorrhiza p. 26, 27

DICOTYLEDONS p. 30

NETTLE FAMILY Urticaceae
Cannabis p. 33
Laportae p. 43
Urtica p. 43
Pilea p. 44
Boehmeria p. 44
BUCKWHEAT FAMILY Polygonaceae
Polygonum p. 35-38
Polygonella p. 37
GOOSEFOOT FAMILY Chenopodiaceae
Salicornia p. 31
Salsola p. 34
AMARANTH FAMILY Amaranthaceae
Amaranthus p. 42
KNOTWORT FAMILY Illecebraceae
Paronychia p. 35

PINK FAMILY Caryophyllaceae
Saponaria p. 55
CROWFOOT FAMILY Ranunculaceae
Thalictrum p. 32
Aconitum p. 46
Cimicifuga p. 46
FUMITORY FAMILY Fumariaceae
Adlumia p. 63
MUSTARD FAMILY Cruciferae
Lepidium p. 58
Capsella p. 58
Cakile p. 57
Sisymbrium p. 58
SUNDEW FAMILY Droseraceae
Drosera p. 59
RIVER WEED FAMILY Podostemaceae
Podostemum p. 31

187

INDEX AND PICTURED GLOSSARY

A

Abutilon
theophrasti, 45
Acalypha
ostryaefolia, 41
virginica, 41
ACHENE: a small dry and hard one-celled one-seeded non-splitting fruit. 10
Aconitum
uncinatum, 46
Actinomeris
alternifolia, 152
ACUMINATE: with the leaf-tip about twice as long as broad. Fig. 496

Figure 496

ACUTE: with the leaf-tip about as long as broad. Fig. 497

Figure 497

Adlumia
fungosa, 63
Aeschynomene
virginica, 65
Agastache
neptoides, 87
scrophulariaefolia, 86
Agrimonia
pubescens, 61
striata, 62
Agrimony, 61, 62
Alisma
subcordatum, 18
Allium
stellatum, 23
Amaranth, 42
Amaranthus
graecizans, 42
hybridus, 42
retroflexus, 42
Ambrosia
artemisiifolia, 132
trifida, 122
American Bugbane, 46
American Cocklebur, 133
American Orpine, 60
American Pennyroyal, 92
American Sea Rocket, 57
Ampelamus
albidus, 72

Amphicarpa
bracteata, 67
Anaphalis
margaritaceae, 136
Annual Salt-marsh Aster, 164
Anthemis
cotula, 154
ANTHER: the pollen bearing part of the stamen. Fig. 498

Figure 498

Antirrhinum
majus, 99
Apios
americana, 65
Arctium
lappa, 138
minus, 138
Arrow Grass, 17
Arrow-head, 18
Arrow-leaved Aster, 161
Arrow-leaved Tear-thumb, 36
Artemisia
caudata, 134
glauca, 134
vulgaris, 134
Artichoke, 186
Asclepias
incarnata, 73
sullivantii, 73
verticillata, 72
Ascyrum
hypericoides, 47
Asiatic Day-flower, 23
Aster
acuminatus, 168
azureus, 160
commutatus, 165
concolor, 164
cordifolius, 160, 161
divaricatus, 158
ericoides, 166
laevis, 163
lateriflorus, 169
linariifolius, 167
macrophyllus, 158
novae-angliae, 161
novi-belgii, 163
patens, 162
praealtus, 170
prenantho des, 162
ptarmicoides, 168
puniceus, 163
sagittifolius, 160
salicifolius, 170
sericeus, 164
shortii, 157
simplex, 169
spectabilis, 165
subulatus, 164
tenuifolius, 164
tradescanti, 166

umbellatus, 167
undulatus, 159
Aster-like Boltonia, 150
Auricled Gerardia, 104
Author, 11
Authority, 11
AWL-SHAPED: tapering upward from the base to a slender point. Fig. 499

Figure 499

AWN: a bristle-like appendage.
AXIL: angle formed by the leaf with the stem. Fig. 500

Figure 500

B

Balsam Apple, 106
Bartonia
paniculata, 76
virginica, 76
Beach Clotbur, 133
Beaked Lygodesmia, 117
Bean, 67, 68
Beech-drops, 54, 82
Beefsteak-plant, 89
Beggar-ticks, 179, 180
Bellflower, 108
Berry, 10
Bidens
aristosa, 181
bipinnata, 179
cernua, 180
connata, 180
coronata, 181
coronata, 182
frondosa, 179
laevis, 181
Biennial Gaura, 53
Binomial System, 11
BIPINNATIFID: twice divided in a pinnate-manner.
Bird-foot Violet, 59
Bishop-weed, 51
Black Bindweed, 36
Black Knapweed, 138
Black Nightshade, 74
Black-eyed Susan, 153
Bladderwort, 82

BLADE: the flat expanded part of a leaf or petal. 6. Fig. 501

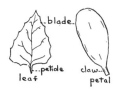

Figure 501

CALYX: the outer whorl of the perianth of a flower, composed of sepals. 7. Fig. 502

Figure 502

Cichorium
  intybus, 112
CILIATE: bearing a marginal fringe of hairs.
Cimicifuga
  americana, 46
Circaea
  alpina, 52
  quadrisulcata, 52
Cirsium
  altissimum, 130
  discolor, 130
  iowense, 130
  muticum, 131
  pumilum, 131
  vulgare, 129
Clammy Cuphea, 56
Clammy Everlasting, 137
Clammy Ground Cherry, 74
Clammy Hedge-hyssop, 101
CLAW: the narrow base of the petal of some flowers. Fig. 504

Figure 504

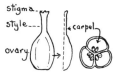

INDEX

Corallorhiza
  maculata, 26
  odontorhiza, 27
Coral-root, 26, 27
CORDATE: heart-shaped.
  Fig. 505

Figure 505

Coreopsis
  tripteris, 151
COROLLA: the inner whorl
  of the perianth of a
  flower, composed of petals. 7. Fig. 506

Figure 506

COTYLEDON: seed-leaf of
  the embryo containing
  stored food.
Cowbane, 51
Creeping Bellflower, 108
Crested Sagittaria, 19
Crooked-stem Aster, 162
Cross-leaved Milkwort, 64
Crotalaria
  sagittalis, 64
Crownbeard, 155
Cucumber, 106
Cudweed, 136
Cuphea
  petiolata, 56
Cup-plant, 157
Curtis' Golden-rod, 174
Curtiss' Milkwort, 64
Cut-leaved Water Hoar-
  hound, 91
Cylindric
  Blazing Star, 139
CYME: a broad flattish in-
  florescence with its cen-
  tral or terminal flowers
  blooming first. Fig. 507

Figure 507

D

Daisy-fleabane, 148
Darwin, 29
Day-flower, 23
Decodon
  verticillatus, 56
DECOMPOUND: more than
  once compounded or di-
  vided.
DECUMBENT: reclining, but
  with the growing ends
  erect.
DEHISCENT: splitting open
  along definite lines at
  maturity, 10.
Dense Blazing Star, 141
Dense-flowered Aster, 165
Desmodium
  canadense, 70
  nudiflorum, 69
  paniculatum, 69
  rotundifolium, 66
Devil's Claw, 98
Dicotyledons, 30
Diodia
  teres, 107
Dioecious, 9
Dipsacus
  sylvestris, 107
DISK-FLOWER: a form of
  flower of the Compositae
  having a tubular corolla;
  also called tube-flower.
  9. Fig. 508

Figure 508

Ditch Stonecrop, 34
Dock, 36
Dotted Button-snakeroot,
  140
Double Golden-rod, 178
Downy False Foxglove, 104
Downy Gentian, 80
Downy Golden-rod, 174
Downy Lobelia, 111
Downy Ragged Golden-
  rod, 172
Downy Rattlesnake
  Plantain, 28
Dragon-head, 88
Drosera
  filiformis, 59
Drummond's Aster, 160
Drummond's Orange-
  grass, 54
Dryer, 12
Drying, 12

E

Eastern Silvery Aster, 164
Eaton's Sagittaria, 19
Echinacea
  angustifolia, 154
  purpurea, 154
Echinocystis
  lobata, 106

Echium
  vulgare, 83   41
Elecampane, 150
Elephantopus
  carolinianus, 141
  nudatus, 142
  tomentosus, 142
Elephant's-foot, 141, 142
ELLIPTIC: oval.
Elm-leaved Golden-rod, 176
EMBRYO: the rudimentary
  plantlet within the seed.
Enchanter's Nightshade, 52
Entire-leaved Rosin-
  wood, 157
EPHEMERAL: lasting but a
  day; very short lived.
Epifagus
  virginiana, 82
Epilobium
  angustifolium, 53
  coloratum, 53
Erechtites
  hieracifolia, 135
Erigeron
  annuus, 147
  canadensis, 147
  divaricatus, 147
  strigosus, 148
Eriocaulon
  decangulare, 21
  septangulare, 21
Eryngium
  yuccifolium, 49
Essential parts, 8
Eupatorium
  album, 128
  altissimum, 128
  aromaticum, 126
  coelestinum, 123
  hyssopifolium, 127
  incarnatum, 125
  lecheaefolium, 127
  perfoliatum, 124
  pilosum, 129
  purpureum, 126
  rugosum, 125
  serotinum, 127
Euphorbia
  corollata, 40
  dentata, 40
  heterophylla, 39
  maculata, 38
  marginata, 39
  polygonifolia, 39
  pulcherrima, 40
  supina, 39
European Vervain, 96
Evening Primrose, 52
Everlasting, 136, 137
EXSERTED: projecting be-
  yond the other parts, as
  with stamens or stigma.

F

Fairy Creeper, 63
Fall Dandelion, 112
Fall White Aster, 169
False Beech-drops, 54
False Boneset, 135
False Buckwheat, 36
False Foxglove, 103
False Nettle, 44
False Pennyroyal, 84
False Pimpernel, 102
Feather-columbine, 32

192

INDEX

Field Milkwort, 64
Field Mint, 90
Field Sow Thistle, 113
Field Thistle, 130
Figwort, 100
Figwort Giant-hyssop, 86
FILAMENT: the stalk of a stamen, 8. Fig. 509

Figure 509

FILIFORM: very slender like a thread.
Fine-leaved Sneeze-weed, 146
Fire-On-The-Mountain, 39
Fireweed, 53, 135
Flat-top White Aster, 167
Fleabane, 142, 148
Flor da Water Parsnip, 50
Flower, 7
Flowering Spurge, 40
Folder, 12
FOLLICLE: a dry fruit of one carpel opening on its ventral side. 10
Forking Whitlow-wort, 35
Foxglove, 103, 104
Fragrant Golden-rod, 170
Fringed Gentian, 78
Frog-spear, 27
Fruit, 10
Fumitory, 63

G

Galinsoga
  caracasana, 145
  ciliata, 145
  parviflora, 145
Gall-of-the-earth, 120
Garden Huckleberry, 74
Garden Lettuce, 115
Garden Phlox, 76
Gaura
  biennis, 53
Gentian, 78-81
Gentiana
  affinis, 80
  andrewsii, 81
  autumnalis, 79
  crinita, 79
  flavida, 80
  procera, 78
  puberula, 80
  quinquefolia, 78
  saponaria, 81
Geranium
  robertianum, 57
Gerardia
  auriculata, 104
  flava, 104
  obtusifolia, 105
  pedicularia, 103
  purpurea, 104
  tenuifolia, 105
  virginica, 103
Giant Sunflower, 184

Giant-hyssop, 86, 87
Glasswort, 31
Glaucous White Lettuce, 119
Gnaphalium
  macounii, 137
  obtusifolium, 137
  uliginosum, 136
Golden Aster, 149
Golden Hedge-hyssop, 101
Golden-glow, 152
Golden-rod, 170-178
Goodyera
  pubescens, 28
Grain, 10
Grass-leaved Golden Aster, 149
Grass-leaved Sagittaria, 19
Grass-leaved Stenanthium, 24
Grass-of-parnassus, 60
Gratiola
  aurea, 101
  virginiana, 101
Gray Golden-rod, 178
Great Lobelia, 110
Great Ragweed, 122
Green Amaranth, 42
Grindelia
  lanceolata, 145
  squarrosa, 145
Ground Cherry, 74, 75
Groundnut, 65
Groundsel, 133
Gum-plant, 145

H

Habenaria
  nivea, 27
HABITAT: a plant's natural place of growth.
Hairy Bush Clover, 71
Hairy Golden Aster, 149
Hairy Golden-rod, 173
Hairy Hawkweed, 118
Hairy Sunflower, 185
Hairy Wood-lettuce, 116
Halberd-leaved Rose Mallow, 47
Halberd-leaved Tear-thumb, 35
Hare Figwort, 100
Hasheesh, 33
HASTATE: like the head of an arrow but with the basal lobes pointing outward, often almost at right angles. Fig. 510

Figure 510

Hatpins, 21
Hawkweed, 117, 119
Hay-fever Weed, 132
Heal-all, 87
Heath Aster, 166

Hedeoma
  pulegioides, 92
Hedge Mustard, 58
Hedge Nettle, 88
Hedge-hyssop, 101
Helenium
  autumnale, 146
  nudiflorum, 146
  tenuifolium, 146
Helianthus
  angustifolius, 182
  annuus, 183
  decopetalus, 184
  divaricatus, 186
  giganteus, 184
  grosse-serratus, 185
  microcephalus, 183
  mollis, 185
  strumosus, 186
  tuberosus, 186
Heliopsis
  helianthoides, 155
  scabra, 155
Hemlock Parsley, 51
Hemlock Water Parsnip, 50
Hemp, 33
Henning, 157
HERBACEOUS: green and leaf-like. 2
Herbarium, 12
Herb Robert, 57
Heteranthera
  dubia, 22
Heterotheca
  subaxillaris, 148
Hibiscus
  militaris, 47
  moscheutos, 47
Hieracium
  canadense, 117
  gronovii, 118
  paniculatum, 119
  scabrum, 118
Hoarhound, 91
Hoary Mountain Mint, 94
Hoary Vervain, 95
Hog-peanut, 67
Hooded Ladies'-tresses, 29
Hornbeam Three-seeded Mercury, 41
Horse Mint, 85
Horse-weed, 122, 147
Husk-tomato, 75
Hymenocallis
  occidentalis, 25
Hypericum
  denticulatum, 49
  drummondii, 54
  gentianoides, 54
  perforatum, 48
  sphaerocarpum, 48
Hyssop Hedge Nettle, 88
Hyssop-leaved Thorough-wort, 127

I

Impatiens
  capensis, 97
  pallida, 97
INDEHISCENT: not opening.
Indian Hemp, 45
Indian Plantain, 136
Indian-tobacco, 111

193

INDEX

INFERIOR OVARY: one that is below the calyx. Fig. 511

Figure 511

INFLORESCENCE: the arrangement of the flowering parts of a plant. 9
Inland Marsh Fleabane, 142
Inula
  helenium, 150
INVOLUCRE: a circle or collection of bracts surrounding a flower or flower cluster, as in the Compositae.
Iowa Thistle, 130
Ironweed, 143, 144
Isanthus
  brachiatus, 84

J

Jerusalem Artichoke, 186
Joê-pye Weed, 126
Jointed Glasswort, 31
Jointweed, 37

K

Keys, 15
Kidney-leaved Grass-of-parnassus, 60
Knotweed, 37
Kuhnia
  eupatorioides, 135

L

Lachnanthes
  tinctoria, 26
Lactuca
  biennis, 114
  canadensis, 115
  hirsuta, 116
  sativa, 115
  scariola, 115
Ladies'-tresses, 28-30
Lady's Thumb, 36
Laportea
  canadensis, 43
Large Button-snakeroot, 140
Large Coral-root, 26
Large Leaved Aster, 158
Large Marsh Pink, 77
Large Spotted Spurge, 38
Large-Leaved Pondweed, 16
Larger
  Bur-marigold, 181
Late Coral-root, 26
Late Flowering Thorough-wort, 127
Late Golden-rod, 177
Late Purple Aster, 162
Leaf, 6
Leaf-cup, 155

LEAFLET: a single division of a compound leaf. 7 Fig. 512

Figure 512

Lechea
  minor, 54
Leontodon
  autumnalis, 112
  leysseri, 112
Lepidium
  virginicum, 58
Lespedeza
  capitata, 71
  hirta, 71
  intermedia, 70
  procumbens, 66
  stuevei, 70
Lettuce, 114-116
Liatris
  cylindracea, 139
  graminifolia, 140
  punctata, 140
  pycnostachya, 139
  scariosa, 140
  spicata, 141
  squarrosa, 139
Lignin, 3
LIGULATE: with strap-shaped corolla as in the ray-flowers of Compositae. 9 Fig. 513

Figure 513

Limonium
  carolinianum, 59
Linaria
  canadensis, 99
  vulgaris, 99
Lindernia
  dubia, 102
Linear-leaved Ladies'-tresses, 28
Linear-leaved Worm-wood, 134
Linnaeus, 11
Lobelia
  cardinalis, 109
  dortmanna, 109
  elongata, 110
  inflata, 111
  kalmii, 111
  puberula, 111
  siphilitica, 110

LOMENT: a jointed legume, usually with constrictions between the seeds. 10 Fig. 514

Figure 514

Long-stalked False Pimpernel, 102
Loose-flowered Button-snakeroot, 140
Loosestrife, 56
Lousewort, 102
Lousewort False Fox-glove, 103
Low Cudweed, 136
Low Horse-weed, 147
Low Rattlesnake-root, 120
Low Showy Aster, 165
Ludwigia
  alternifolia, 52
Lycopus
  americanus, 91
  rubellus, 92
  virginicus, 92
Lygodesmia
  juncea, 116
  rostrata, 117

M

Mad-dog Skullcap, 84
Many-flowered Psoralea, 68
Marigold, 178
Marijuana, 33
Marjoram, 93
Marrubium
  vulgare, 91
Marsh Fleabane, 142
Marsh Pink, 77
Maryland Figwort, 100
Maryland Golden Aster, 149
Maryland Meadow-beauty, 56
Maryland Milkwort, 64
Mayweed, 154
Meadow-beauty, 56
Meadow-rue, 32
Melanthium
  virginicum, 24
MEMBRANOUS: thin, soft, pliable and more or less translucent.
Mentha
  arvensis, 90
  piperita, 91
  spicata, 90
Mexican Fire-plant, 39
Mikania
  scandens, 122
Milk Purslane, 39
Milkweed, 72, 73
Milkwort, 64
Mint, 85, 90, 91, 93, 94
Mist Flower, 123

INDEX

Figure 515

Figure 516

OVULE: the body which after fertilization becomes the seed.

P

PALMATE: lobed or divided like the fingers on a hand. 7. Fig. 517

Figure 517

PANICLE: a compound raceme; an inflorescence in which the lateral branches rebranch. Fig. 518

Figure 518

PAPPUS: the modified calyx in Compositae borne at the summit of the achene. 10 Fig. 519

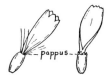

Figure 519

PEDICEL: the stalk of a single flower in a flower-cluster. 7 Fig. 520

Figure 520

PEDUNCLE: the main stalk of a single flower or of a flower-cluster. 7
Perfect flower, 8
PERENNIAL: a plant that lives for more than two seasons, usually many years.
PERIANTH: the floral envelope; both calyx and corolla considered together, especially when they are very similar. 8
PETAL: one of the divisions of the corolla.

INDEX

PETIOLE: the stalk of the leaf. 6 Fig. 521

Figure 521

Phaseolus
  polystachios, 67
Phlox
  paniculata, 76
Photosynthesis, 4
Physalis
  heterophylla, 74
  lanceolata, 75
  virginiana, 75
Physostegia
  virginiana, 88
Pickerel-weed, 22
Pickle-plant, 31
Pig-Potato, 51
Pilea
  pumila, 44
Pimpernel, 102
Pinesap, 54
Pink Thoroughwort, 125
PINNATE: feather-like arrangement. 7 Fig. 522

Figure 522

PINNATIFID: cleft or divided in a pinnate manner.
Pin-weed, 54
Pipewort, 21
PISTIL: the seed-bearing part of the flower consisting of ovary and stigma and style when present. 7 Fig. 523

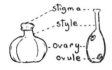

Figure 523

PISTILLATE: having female parts (pistils) only. 9
PLACENTA: any part of the interior of the ovary which bears ovules. 6

PLAIT: a fold or appendage, especially in the corolla. Fig. 524

Figure 524

Plantago
  lanceolata, 73
Plantain, 18, 28
Plant Groups, 2
Plant Processes, 4
Pluchea
  camphorata, 142
  petiolata, 142
POD: any dry fruit that splits open. 10
Podostemum
  ceratophyllum, 31
Poinsettia, 40
POLLEN: the powdery contents of an anther; the essential male cells.
Pollination, 5
Polygala
  cruciata, 64
  curtissii, 64
  mariana, 64
  nuttallii, 64
Polygonella
  articulata, 37
Polygonum
  arifolium, 35
  coccineum, 38
  sagittatum, 36
  scandens, 36
Polymnia
  canadensis, 155
Pondweed, 16
Pontederia
  cordata, 22
Potamogeton
  amplifolius, 16
Prairie Aster, 165
Prairie Burdock, 156
Prairie Button-snake-root, 139
Prairie Dock, 156
Prairie False Boneset, 135
Prairie Ground Cherry, 75
Prairie Ironweed, 143
Prairie Pink, 117
Prairie Wild Onion, 23
Prenanthes
  alba, 120
  altissima, 120
  nana, 120
  racemosa, 119
  trifoliata, 120
Pressing, 12
Prickly Lettuce, 115
Prince's Feather, 36
Proboscidea
  louisiana, 98
Prostrate Tick-trefoil, 66

Prunella
  vulgaris, 87
Psoralea
  tenuiflora floribunda, 68
Ptilimnium
  capillaceum, 51
  costatum, 51
Purple Aster, 162
Purple Bladderwort, 82
Purple Cone-flower, 154
Purple Gerardia, 104
Purple-headed Sneeze-weed, 146
Purple-leaved Willow-herb, 53
Purple-stemmed Swamp Beggar-tick, 180
Purslane Speedwell, 101
Pycnanthemum
  flexuosum, 94
  incanum, 94
  virginianum, 93

Q

Queen's Delight, 41

R

RACEME: an inflorescence as pictured. Fig. 525

Figure 525

Ragged Golden-rod, 172
Ragweed, 122, 132
Rattle-box, 64
Rattlesnake Master, 49
Rattlesnake Plantain, 28
Rattlesnake Root, 120
RAY-FLOWER: a flower of the Compositae with strap-shaped corolla; usually borne on the margin of the head. 9 Fig. 526

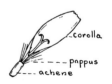

Figure 526

INDEX

RECEPTACLE: the tip of the flower-stalk on which the floral parts are attached. 7 **Fig. 527**

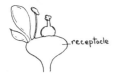

Figure 527

SAGITTATE: shaped like an arrowhead. **Fig. 528**

Figure 528

SESSILE: without a stalk. **Fig. 529**

Figure 529

Seven-angled Pipewort, 21
Sharp-toothed Golden-rod, 176
SHEATH: a tubular envelope surrounding part of the stem as in Polygonaceae. Fig. 530

Figure 530

Red-leaved Wood Sorrel, 61
Red-robin, 57
Red-root, 26
Red-stalk Aster, 163
Red-turtlehead, 100
Reference Books, 14
Rein-orchid, 27
RENIFORM: kidney shaped.
Respiration, 5
Rhexia
  mariana, 56
  virginica, 56
Rhubarb, 36
Rib Grass, 73
Rich-weed, 89
Ricinus
  communis, 41
River-weed, 31
Rose Mallow, 47
Rosin-plant, 156
Rosin-weed, 157
Rosin-wood, 157
Round-headed Bush Clover, 71
Round-podded St. John's-wort, 48
Rough Buttonweed, 107
Rough Hawkbit, 112
Rough Hawkweed, 118
Rough Leaved Golden-rod, 176
Rough Ox-eye, 155
Rough Pigweed, 42
Rough Sunflower, 186
Rudbeckia
  fulgida, 153
  hirta, 153
  laciniata, 152
  subtomentosa, 153
  triloba, 153
Rush-like Lygodesmia, 116
Russian Thistle, 34

S

Sabatia
  dodecandra, 77
  stellaris, 77
Sagittaria
  cristata, 19
  eatoni, 19
  graminea, 19
  latifolia, 18

St. Andrew's Cross, 47
St. John's-wort, 48, 49
Salicornia
  europaea, 31
SALINE: salty.
Salsola
  kali tenuifolia, 34
Salt-marsh Aster, 164
Salt-marsh Fleabane, 142
Saltwort, 31
Samara, 10
Samphire, 31
Sand Vine, 72
Sanguisorba
  canadensis, 32
  officinalis, 32
Saponaria
  officinalis, 55
SAPROPHYTE: a plant which derives its food from dead plants or animals.
Saw-toothed Sunflower, 185
SCALE: a small or rudimentary leaf-like body.
Scaly Blazing Star, 139
SCAPE: a peduncle that arises from the ground, leafless but sometimes with scales or bracts.
Schizocarp, 10
Scratchgrass, 35
Scrophularia
  lanceolata, 100
  marilandica, 100
Scutellaria
  lateriflora, 84
Sea Lavender, 59
Sea Pink, 77
Sea Rocket, 57
Seaside Arrow Grass, 17
Sea-side Golden-rod, 175
Seaside Spurge, 39
Sedum
  telephioides, 60
  triphyllum, 60
Seed, 10
Seedbox, 52
Senecio
  vulgaris, 133
Sensitive Joint Vetch, 65
Sensitive Plant, 62
SEPAL: one of the divisions of the calyx.
SERRATE: having sharp teeth which point forward.

Sheep Sorrel, 36
Shepherd's Purse, 58
Shore Spurge, 39
Short's Aster, 159
Showy Aster, 165
Showy Golden-rod, 174
Showy Tick-trefoil, 70
Sickle-leaved Golden Aster, 149
Sicyos
  angulatus, 106
Silique, 10
Silphium
  integrifolium, 157
  laciniatum, 156
  perfoliatum, 157
  terebinthinaceum, 156
  trifoliatum, 157
Silver-rod, 171
Silver-weed, 171
Sisymbrium
  officinale, 58
Sium
  floridanum, 50
  suave, 50
Skullcap, 84
Sky-blue Aster, 160
Slender Fragrant Golden-rod, 170
Slender Gerardia, 105
Slender Ladies'-tresses, 29
Slender Pigweed, 42
Slender Wild Nettle, 43
Slender Yellow-eyed Grass, 20
Small Wood Sunflower, 183
Small Yellow Crown-beard, 155
Small-flowered Ladies'-tresses, 30
Small-flowered Leaf-cup, 155
Small-headed Bushy Golden-rod, 171

197

INDEX

SPADIX: a spike with a
  fleshy axis.
SPATULATE: somewhat
  spoon-shaped. Fig. 531

Figure 531

SPIKE: an inflorescence with
  sessile flowers arranged
  along the stem. Fig. 532

Figure 532

STAMEN: the pollen-bear-
  ing, male organ of the
  flower. 7
STAMINATE: bearing only
  male parts (stamens). 9
STIGMA: the part of the
  pistil which receives the
  pollen. 8 Fig. 533

Figure 533

STIPULE: a leaf-like ap-
  pendage at the base of
  the leafstalk. 6 Fig. 534

Figure 534

STYLE: the part of the pistil that connects the
  ovary and stigma. 8
  Fig. 535

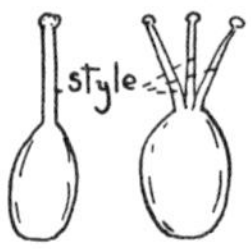

Figure 535

SUCCULENT: juicy, fleshy.
SUPERIOR OVARY: one that
  is above the calyx and
  free from it. Fig. 536

Figure 536

INDEX